OPEN YOUR HEART

with

Quilting

*"*Kelly Smith has written a wonderfully inspiring book for all Quilters. It also reaffirms the creative path I and other quilters have chosen.*"*

—M'Liss Rae Hawley, the award-winning author
of eleven quilting books and the host of the PBS series
M'Liss's World of Quilts. She is the official spokesperson
for Husqvarna Viking Sewing Machines and
Robison-Anton Textiles Company.

*"*I believe that quilting is much more than making a quilt. It represents the heart of the maker. Many people see quilts as utilitarian—and they are. However, you will see by reading these pages that they are also therapeutic, inspirational, and emotional. Kelly Smith has opened her heart to show us how versatile and important quilting is to the lives of the quilters, as well as those who benefit from their work. By reading this book you will no doubt discover how powerful quilting is—can be— has been for me!*"*

—Ricky Tims, known just about equally for his music
and his quilting. Ricky has published several quilting books
and patterns and has his own line of fabric.
He has also released several CDs.

OPEN YOUR HEART

with

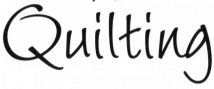

Mastering Life through Love of the Patches

KELLY SMITH

DreamTime Publishing, Inc.

DreamTime Publishing, Inc., books are available at special quantity discounts for bulk purchases for sales promotions, premiums, fund-raising, and educational needs. Please contact us at www.DreamTimePublishing.com for additional information.

Library of Congress Cataloging-in-Publication Data

Smith, Kelly (Kelly M.)
  Open your heart with quilting : mastering life through love of the stitches / Kelly Smith.
    p. cm.
    ISBN 978-1-60166-014-5 (trade pbk.)
    1. Quilting. 2. Quilting—Patterns 3. Quilting—Psychological aspects. I. Title.

TT835.S55498   2008
746.46'041—dc22

2008018388

Printed in the United States of America.

Branding, website, and cover design for DreamTime Publishing by
    Rearden Killion * www.reardenkillion.com
Illustrations by Janice Marie Phelps * www.janicephelps.com
Manuscript consulting by Jeannette Cézanne * www.customline.com
Text layout and design by Gary A. Rosenberg * www.garyarosenberg.com

This publication is designed to provide accurate and authoritative information in regard to the subject matter covered. It is sold with the understanding that the publisher is not engaged in rendering legal, accounting, or other professional service. If legal advice or other expert assistance is required, the services of a competent professional person should be sought.

—From a declaration of principles jointly adopted by a committee of the American Bar Association and a committee of publishers.

This book is printed on recycled, acid-free paper containing a minimum of 50% recycled, de-inked fiber.

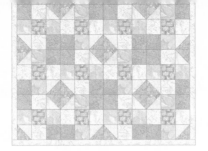

Contents

Note from the Publisher

Balancing the overall mission of a series of books with each author's individual creativity and vision is an enjoyable and rewarding challenge. The goal of this note is to tie the loose ends together to make your experience with this book as meaningful as possible.

We have two goals with the Open Your Heart series. The first is to provide you with practical advice about your hobby or interest, in this case quilting. We trust this advice will increase your ongoing enjoyment of quilting or even encourage you to explore a new activity.

Our second goal is to help you use what you know and love to make the rest of your life happier and easier. This process worked in different ways for each of our writers, so it will likely work in different ways for each of you. For some, it's a matter of becoming more self-aware. Just realizing what makes you happy while immersed in creating a new project, and then gradually learning to use those feelings as a barometer when dealing with your job, relationships, and other issues could be an important first step. For others, quilting provides an important outlet for stress and contemplation, allowing you to go back into your daily life refreshed. For yet others, you might discover how to meditate, how to connect with the mysterious flow of the Universe when you are immersed in quilting. Once you recognize the beauty of that for what it is, you can then learn to connect with the flow in other ways at other times.

We are not suggesting you will find all of your answers in this book. We are, though, inviting you to look at something you love with new eyes, a new perspective, and a new heart. Once you recognize the importance of feeling good in one area of your life, you are open to feeling good in the rest of your life. And that is the cornerstone to mastering your life.

Happy reading!

Meg Bertini
Publisher

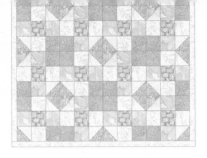

Acknowledgements

Many people helped create this book. As you can see from the large number of quotes in the text, it was not a solitary effort. I would like to extend my thanks to each of my contributors, friend and stranger alike, to the professional quilters and amateurs (like me), to the novices and the experienced quilters who each took time to talk to me or write down answers to a long list of questions. You all gave your unique perspective on why you quilt, and I hope that our collective passion for the art shines through as intended.

I would also like to thank my quilting friends who encouraged me and cheered me on throughout the research, writing, and editing process. Their support and excitement about this project really helped sustain my own enthusiasm. They are a huge part of why I love quilting and this book would not exist if I had not found such a warm welcome in the quilting community.

Finally, I would like to thank my editor Jeannette Cézanne for cleaning up all the mistakes and offering her help and advice before the book was even official!

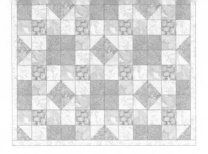

Author's Note

I have a dear friend who just didn't get it—mostly with regard to the hand stitching I enjoy. He enjoys spending the day fishing—which I didn't really understand. In the process of him teaching me to fish, I was able to take his explanations of the Zen of fishing and flip that to help him understand the Zen of quilting. Many a day we sat at the river's edge and he fished while I quilted.

—DEBBIE KRUEGER

Doesn't this sound idyllic? It does to me. Not everyone will understand why you quilt, and you can waste a lot of breath trying to explain it to others. Unless they have a passion of their own (as Debbie's friend did), they probably won't understand why you spend thousands of dollars on equipment and fabric only to make something that to them may not look like much more than a blanket.

Another quilter and founding member of my quilting bee who responded to my call, Adrienne Alexander, had her own fish tale to tell. "Many years ago I used to scoff and make fun of men that I knew who would enjoy ice fishing as a hobby. I would point out that there was nothing more ridiculous than drilling a hole in the ice and then staring into it for hours at a time while freezing certain body parts in the process. Just didn't make any sense to me. Then I began to shop and pay ten dollars a yard for fabric. I brought it home, I washed it, I ironed it, I cut it into little pieces, and then I sewed it all back together again. Hmm . . . now I *never* say anything about anyone else's hobbies!"

So as you see, "fun" is all in the eyes of the beholder. *Open Your Heart with Quilting* will attempt to explain (through plenty of examples) why people quilt, and what exactly they get out of the process. The reasons are many and varied, and I have tried to get a broad representation of quilters. I have spoken to people of all ages and both genders from all over the United States, and a few from other parts of the world as well. Some of these people will be known to you from their award-winning quilts, books, classes, patterns, fabric lines, and websites. Some of them are completely anonymous at their request, and a lot of them are just "ordinary" artists, toiling away alone, seeking that elusive moment when the world slips away and their hands bring forth an unexpected masterpiece.

In addition to helping you reach that kind of "Zen" state that Debbie talks about, I hope the book will help explain to non-quilters why we are compelled to do what we do. (And honestly, I hope it encourages some of them to become quilters too! If there is one things quilters love, it is passing the passion on to others.)

One thing I should clear up right upfront is that not all quilters are little old ladies in rocking chairs straining their eyes while they make perfect hand-quilting stitches on an heirloom quilt. Quilters (even the "little old ladies" I know) are a vibrant, creative, fun, and varied group.

Many men quilt, and at least one popular quilting magazine, Mark Lipinski's *Quilter's Home*, is edited by a man. Quilting is a universal art form that anyone can enjoy. Children quilt, both for

school projects and on their own with their families. Mentally and physically disabled people also benefit from the meditative, creative aspects of quilting.

There are even some ergonomic quilting tools designed for those who may not be able to easily manipulate traditional quilting tools, or for those who want to prevent repetitive stress injuries. There are sewing machines that use a knee lift instead of a lever moved by hand, and rotary cutters designed to be used while seated instead of requiring the user to be standing and bent over a surface.

People's reasons for quilting are as different as the quilters themselves, but at the core of it is a passion for sharing an inner vision with the world at large. Judy Martin says, "I am driven to capture my emotional responses to the world around me in fiber. Whether it is celebration or sadness, anger or grief, there is often a quilt that has to be made."

As I was writing this book, I solicited feedback from a group of about thirty-five quilters with whom I go on retreat twice a year. I also sent questionnaires to many quilters from the Sacred Threads show in Reynoldsburg, Ohio, and left a stack of them at the show for other quilters to find. I announced the book at my local quilt guild meeting and got feedback from several people there. I also thought of every "famous" quilter whose work I enjoy, and I contacted as many of them as I could for interviews. A few could not participate, but many did, and their words are in these pages along with dozens of lesser-known or completely unknown quilters. They are from all walks of life and represent a wide range of ages and worldviews. I hope that their stories will be as inspiring to you as they were to me.

We each come to quilting for our own reasons and with our own preferences.

Some rare types enjoy every aspect of quilting. Others, like me, enjoy some parts of it more than other parts. I compare it to baking. I love to bake. But I don't necessarily love *every* aspect of baking. Measuring is tedious; waiting for something to bake is boring. Sometimes you just want to skip the last step and eat the cookie dough raw!

I find some parts of quilting boring too. I am excited by design and color choice, piecing and revealing the finished quilt top. The actual quilting of the layers together is boring to me and I only do it when I have to. To me, quilting a quilt top is like baking the cookies—an optional step that I only do if I'm quilting (or baking) for someone else. For my own enjoyment, a finished quilt top (or a bowl of dough) is more than enough to satisfy!

I hope that this book helps you find which part of quilting opens *your* heart and satisfies *you*. If you realize that you love every aspect, more power to you, but even if you end up just loving one particular aspect more than the others, that doesn't make you any less of a quilter, and you will be one step closer to opening your heart with quilting.

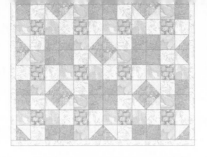

Preface

Learning to live in the present moment is part of the path of joy.
—SARAH BAN BREATHNACH

For the past several years I have been trying various methods of living in the present moment. When I was suffering from anxiety disorder, reading and rereading Breathnach's *Simple Abundance* books helped me to approach each day as an opportunity to deepen my understanding of what it took to be my authentic self and to appreciate all that I had. My anxiety was rooted in worrying about every little detail of things over which I had absolutely no control. Following her simple instructions and focusing on what I *could* control—my own thoughts and actions—helped me immeasurably, and I read her meditations every day for two years until I reached a point where I thought I could continue on my own without the daily reminders.

I find myself drifting off the path, though—letting the stress of work and life get to me (especially now as I take a vacation day from my day job in order to write this book, whose deadline is looming). But her words come back to me at odd times, especially as I read the words of the contributors to this book. Each of these artists is unique, but more importantly, they are authentic. They are true to themselves in their art.

Each in her own way, they use their passion for quilting to help express whatever it is inside her that is screaming to come out. Just yesterday I found this sentence in an article by Eli Leon on the quilts of Rosie Lee Tompkins. It refers to Rosie's quilting style, which very much resembles the style of improvisation used by the Asante tribe in Africa:

> To the Asante, artistic pursuits are believed to be guided by something more powerful than the individual, and improvisation involves achieving the highest level of communication with oneself.

I think that pretty well describes the focus of this book. Nearly all the quilters who shared their stories indicated that they believe their creativity is "guided by something more powerful than the individual." Some of them attribute this to the traditional God of the Christian and Jewish faiths, others to a pagan goddess, still others to the ineffable energy of the universe. All of them have improvised at one time or another, stumbling sometimes blindly, sometimes with only a vague idea of where they were going with an idea until suddenly, there it was—the finished quilt—a work of art that seemed to be created without much conscious thought on their part. And what did that unique work of art express? Their inner selves—whatever they were feeling at the moment, poured out in fabric and thread.

It was only after reading all their stories and thinking about my own that I remembered Breathnach and her mantra of finding your authentic self. Because that is what each of the artists featured in this book have done. They have allowed the stress and rush of the world to fade into the background, listened to

that still, small voice inside them, and out of the depths of their souls have created beautiful and powerful images based, not on any rules handed down by the Quilt Police, but on their authentic selves. That is the definition of an artist: one who listens to her inner voices and expresses what she hears. And all of these artists have found a way to live in the present moment. They have found the path of joy.

> An artist is merely someone with good listening skills who accesses the creative energy of the Universe to bring forth something on the material plane that wasn't there before. It was a part of Spirit before we could see it.
>
> —Sarah Ban Breathnach

As Roslyn Besterman, another of my contributors, says, "Meditation and prayer are part of the whole process before, during, and when I'm stuck. It's not so much positive thoughts as it is letting go of control and letting spirit guide. It's a listening process and a willingness to go with the flow. When in the flow, I feel excitement and exceeding joy. The piece is no longer mine. It becomes a co-creation."

Roslyn was definitely in the moment. She wasn't fussing about perfect points or color choices. She wasn't worrying what her quilting friends or a show judge would think of her piece. She wasn't agonizing over her stitches. She let go of control. She became an instrument of spirit and, out of that, her quilt was born. Roslyn's story of how her quilt Order out of Chaos was created is remarkable. She was kind enough to share it and you will find it in the section titled "Quilts That are Meant to Be." I think it is a remarkable example of the universe using an artist to create something that has to be created.

I hope that this book will show you how to communicate with *your* authentic self and let the spirit guide you to use that connection to help you birth a beautiful quilt that says something your soul longs to say. It could be any emotion at all—as long as it is authentic, it will be beautiful.

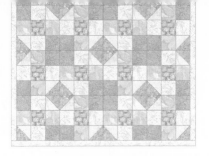

Foreword

Why do we quilters do what we do? I caught myself grinning in recognition at the bewilderment embodied in the question, "Why do you buy expensive fabric, cut it up, and sew it back together again?" Kelly's reply resonates in my soul: "at the core of it is a passion for sharing an inner vision with the world at large."

In *Open Your Heart with Quilting,* Kelly does a fantastic job of reaching across the boundaries of geography, ethnicity, age, education, experience, expertise, and even time itself to glean insights from a fascinating cross-section of the quilting community. This is truly an "insider's look" into the world of quilting and quilt makers—in all our endless, wonderful diversity.

Our quilts have the potential to become an expression of our deepest, most private selves. They also have the potential to celebrate that which is greater than any single individual; they can provide a conduit for the creative energy that seeks to fill us, heal us, and join us to each other just as securely as we join our fabrics with thread. Paradoxically, the more authentically our innermost selves are reflected, the more truly universal the work becomes.

Through a wonderful overview that follows the history of quilting from ancient quilted garments and textiles to well-loved (and often well-worn) bed coverings to fine art displayed in prestigious galleries—and everything in between—Kelly makes the point that all of our quiltmaking efforts are inherently of value, no matter what the end result. The process is as important— sometimes even more important—than the product. However, the product is not to be underestimated! There is joy in the tactile nature of a quilt, however simply it may be constructed. There is power in the deliberate placement of fabrics and stitching. The gift of a custom-made, hand-crafted quilt (whether sewn by hand or machine) is a tangible expression of deliberate generosity of spirit.

Kelly's conversational style allows us to eavesdrop on conversations with well-known celebrities and long-time friends. Very personal motivations involving healing, wholeness, grounding, spirituality, celebration, milestone-marking, legacy, empowerment, activism, and commitment to community are all explored. But it doesn't stop there! In *Open Your Heart with Quilting,* Kelly not only invites you to do just that, but also gives you concrete tips for getting started and useful resources for continuing on. There is a treasure-trove of links and other information to help you connect with charities, educational organizations, and like-minded groups. There are even frank discussions regarding how and when one might turn a love of quilting into a source of income. Finally, there are comprehensive instructions for making a quilt—not by following a rigid construct, but by learning the whys and hows that will allow each person to make choices that most clearly reflect their own personal vision.

I am honored to have been part of Kelly's creative journey. It has been a great pleasure to watch her skills blossom and unfold over the years that I have known her. Her infectious humor and inquisitive, playful, adventurous spirit make her a joy to know.

I am delighted to whole-heartedly recommend this book to all quilters, would-be quilters, and all who ask the question "Why do you *do* that?" Kelly's warm and accessible manner invites all to truly *Open Your Heart with Quilting.*

—Beth Ann Williams

Introduction

I quilt because I must.

—JUDY WHITE

I have been a quilter for more than ten years. I have seventy-one books in my quilting studio that tell me *how* to quilt. I don't have a single one that answers the question I am asked most often by non-quilters: *Why* do you quilt?

Many people associate quilting with little old ladies sitting around a quilt frame. While that may happen from time to time, I've never done it personally, and at not-quite-forty, I don't think I fall into the "little old lady" category—at least, not yet! Others ask me (in all seriousness), "Why do you buy expensive fabric, cut it up, and sew it back together again?" Still others ask how long I've been "knitting" quilts and are puzzled when I tell them I don't know how to knit.

In the past, quilting was a necessity—families needed warm blankets for the winter, and scraps of clothing and household linens were pressed into service as patches to make them—but over the years, quilting has morphed into more than a necessity, bypassed *hobby*, and leapt straight into *obsession* for many people. Young and old, male and female, quilters come from all walks of life and they are inspired and motivated by far more than just a cozy place to sleep.

Quilting was a common pastime in America's history, practiced by men as well as women. There is even at least one quilter among the ranks of U.S. presidents: Calvin Coolidge. According to Michelle Newman in *American Patchwork & Quilting*, young Calvin hand pieced a seventy-eight-inch tumbling blocks quilt with his mother's help when he was about ten years old. The quilt is preserved at the Coolidge family homestead, and there's a link to a picture in the Resources section at the back of this book.

According to the Quilting in America 2006 survey by *Quilter's Newsletter Magazine*, there are more than twenty-seven million quilters in the United States who collectively spend $2.9 million per year on quilting. Most of these quilters are women, and their average age is fifty-nine. They spend an average of $2,304 every year on quilting and buy an average of five quilt books per year.

These people are already deeply interested in quilting, and for some of them (those the survey calls "dedicated quilters") it has moved far beyond a mere hobby. Dedicated quilters make up just 4.7 percent of these twenty-seven million quilters (still a healthy 1,269,000 people), yet they spend 88 percent of the total money spent on quilting. Spending by dedicated quilters has increased 34.6 percent since 2003.

I am one of these dedicated quilters. I have been a quilter for more than ten years. My first and best teacher was Beth Ann Williams. She encouraged me to follow my heart and make what I wanted, not necessarily what some mass-produced pattern said I should. Beth Ann is an inspiration to me and to many other quilters (and non-quilters) who are lucky enough to know her. She overcame being bedridden with multiple sclerosis by taking an interest in her grandmother's quilting. Now she writes books, lectures, teaches, and facilitates creativity retreats. Her quilts hang in homes, offices, and art galleries. She has not let her illness get the better of her and has found ways to work around it and continue quilting. When I first heard of the *Open Your Heart* series, I knew quilting was an ideal subject and that Beth Ann (and the other amazing quilters I know) would be perfect contributors to the book. I already knew they would have a lot to say on the subject of why they quilt.

From my own experience, I know that as my technical skills improved, I became interested in other aspects of quilting. There are only so many techniques to learn and only so many kinds of patterns to try. Eventually you ask yourself, "Why am I spending all this money? What is the point of this?" Many quilters I know quilt not just for the sheer love of colors, designs, and fabric, but also for the deep feeling of purpose and contentment it gives them. Some create gifts, some create works of art, some make quilts for charity or to display in their places of worship, or to express deep grief, joy, frustration, or longing. Once you get past the phase of *fun new hobby*, quilting—like any other art—takes on added dimension and emotional meaning.

Open Your Heart with Quilting will explore the many ways that quilting can enrich your life. The age-old art of quilting can help you connect with your family and community, help you carry on traditions of the past, help you heal from illness or grief, help you celebrate milestones in your life, explore your creativity, deepen your spiritual connection to the universe, and leave a legacy for generations to come. It could even win you fame and fortune!

Open Your Heart with Quilting will explore how you (yes, you) can do any or all of these things . . . and have a great time doing it. Together we will learn about the history of quilting and how (and why) it has been used all around the world for centuries. We will meet some fascinating people whose love of quilting has enriched their lives immeasurably. I will give you easy steps for learning to quilt, and ideas for how to explore this fun and addictive art form.

Through interviews and stories, I will help you open *your* heart with quilting and start you on your own quilting odyssey.

ONE

What Is a Quilt?

Blankets wrap you in warmth,
quilts wrap you in love.
—ANONYMOUS

You may have grown up with quilts around your house. Perhaps your grandmothers or aunts made them. Maybe they were inherited, or found in an old trunk in the attic. If you grew up in the United States, there was probably at least one quilt in your household. It may have been basic or elaborate, pristine or in tatters, but I'm sure it was well loved and well used.

A soft, warm quilt is the perfect thing to snuggle under on a cold night, but quilts can be more than mere utilitarian objects. They can be heirlooms, passed down from generation to generation with great reverence paid to their care. They can be fun, dramatic, and beautiful multimedia artworks incorporating beads, paint, crystals, found objects, and exquisite hand or machine stitching.

They can also be more than just a bedcover. All sorts of items can be quilted, from clothing and fashion accessories (jackets, purses, tote bags, and vests) to home decor items (table runners, wall hangings, and pillows) to artwork and public memorials like the AIDS quilt and the 9/11 quilt.

There are whole museums devoted to quilts, such as MAQS, the Museum of the American Quilter's Society in Paducah, Kentucky. There are quilts hanging in traditional museums that are considered fine art in their own right, such as those on display at the Metropolitan Museum of Art, and those of historical importance like those at the Smithsonian. All of these things are quilts, and each inspires the quilt maker and the quilt viewer in different ways.

This chapter will discuss all the different kinds of quilts and will discuss why different types of quilts are made. People use the art of quilting to connect with family and community (through giving quilts as gifts or donating them to a cause), to carry on traditions of the past and leave a legacy for future generations, to help heal from illness or grief by depicting their sorrows and pains in a visual way, or to celebrate milestones in life such as birthdays, anniversaries, weddings, and graduations.

Some people create devotional quilts or quilted banners for religious and spiritual groups. The methodic acts of cutting, piecing, and quilting lend themselves easily to meditation and prayer.

Quilting can help you to explore your creativity by diverging from published patterns and creating something unique. If a pattern or technique is very novel, it could even win you fame and fortune if you have the energy and personality to write and publish quilt patterns and books, or teach quilting classes.

First though, let's define *quilt* as I am using the word. Merriam-Webster defines a quilt as:

> **1 a:** a bed coverlet of two layers of cloth filled with padding (as down or batting) held in place by ties or stitched designs.
> **b:** Patchwork quilt (a quilt made of patchwork)

2: something that is quilted or resembles a quilt (a quilt of houses and parks)

I personally think the authors are limiting themselves by referring only to bedcovers, but that *is* the most common type of quilt in the United States, so that's where we'll start our exploration. After that, we'll take a look at the other kinds of quilts and quilted items that are popular, and touch on some of the reasons why people make each kind of quilt.

One who sleeps under a quilt is comforted by love.
—ANONYMOUS

Bedcovers

Bed quilts may range from small quilts made for cribs all the way up to quilts that fit king-sized beds. The top layer of a quilt is normally pieced of many different fabrics. Historically in the United States, these pieces were leftover scraps from sewing projects, or from worn-out clothing or other household textiles, including feed sacks and linens. These quilts (often called "patchwork" quilts) usually followed a published pattern, and many American newspapers carried regular quilting columns, some that included quite intricate patterns.

But in many cases, no commercial pattern was followed, and pieces of cloth were just sewn together without following any set pattern. Despite the apparent randomness of their design, some of these "rustic" quilts are now seen as works of art all on their own because of their dramatic use of color and the modern look that resulted from this method.

An example of this rustic technique can be seen in the quilts made by a group of former slaves in a town called Gee's Bend,

Alabama. Six generations of former slaves passed down the quilting tradition and, in 2002, books, exhibits, and documentaries were made based on the women and their quilts. These quilts have even been featured on postage stamps from the U.S. Postal Service. This method is similar to the "crazy quilts" that were popular during the Victorian era, but they were much more utilitarian and did not feature the elaborate hand embroidery and embellishment that made crazy quilts the original art quilts.

In most modern quilts the fabrics are selected not out of necessity or frugality, but for their color, value, or visual texture. They are then cut and sewn together to make a particular pattern. Thousands of quilt patterns exist, and many of them have colorful names and histories.

Some quilt blocks are named after historical figures, such as the block Burgoyne Surrounded (named after Major General Burgoyne, defeated by George Washington). Some are named after events, such as the World's Fair block, and some are named after what they resemble, such as the Mariner's Compass or the Log Cabin.

> Every quilt pattern is a collection of one or more quilt blocks. Quilt blocks are the basic shapes used in a quilt design. Like miniature mosaics they can be made of many smaller shapes sometimes called patches.

Some blocks and patterns were purportedly used as secret clues to aid runaway slaves. Houses displaying quilts with certain designs were considered safe, and sometimes quilts were designed and hung in such as way as to point out a safe route. There is much debate about this theory and many in the quilt world no longer believe that this is historically accurate; in any case, it's a well-known story, and many popular books have been written about it.

Some bed quilts are whole-cloth quilts, where two large sheets of fabric are sewn together with decorative stitching. In these quilts, the stitching itself forms the design. In some of them, sections of quilt between the stitching are stuffed with threads, fibers, or batting so that they puff out, forming a raised pattern called *trapunto*. According to quilt.com, this style of quilt "originated in Italy in the early 16th century. It appeared in the United States in the late 1700s and remained popular until the Civil War."

Other quilts use a technique called appliqué, in which shaped pieces of fabric are sewn onto a plain background to create a scene. Appliqué is a French word that means "to put on." This method allows for a huge range of unique designs and is often used in art quilts because it allows the quilter to depict on the quilt anything he or she can draw in two dimensions, or shape from fabric and other objects. Appliqué quilts may be very traditional and precise like Baltimore Album quilts, or can be naive looking with raw-edge appliqué and simple design.

Bed quilts can be made sturdy enough for everyday use and modern washing machines, or they may be used only for special occasions (such as for company or at Christmastime). They can be made by hand or machine, or a combination of both, and can be absolutely any color, size, or style. That's the great thing about quilts—they are limited only by your imagination!

Art Quilts

Art reveals one's soul . . . It cracks open the solid way we go about our daily lives, gives a glimmer into transcendence.

—MARY ANN TITUS

Art quilts are quilts that are made purely for their aesthetic beauty. They may be functional—as bedcovers, table runners, or clothing—but they generally do not follow a published pattern.

Many art quilts are not pieced at all, relying instead on appliqué, thread painting, hand dying, painting, beading, and other embellishment techniques to create the pattern. Normally the artist drafts his or her own design, and often has to invent novel methods for achieving the desired look. These innovations sometimes move into the "traditional" quilting world and become the common method, especially when they make things faster or easier!

Gayle Pritchard, in *Uncommon Threads: Ohio's Art Quilt Revolution*, discusses the resurgence of interest in art after the end of World War II and how the concept of art expanded to include

Dreamies Descending a Staircase

textiles. Many quilters of that period were weavers first, and the movement from art to quilting was well underway by the 1970s.

That's how Caryl Bryer Fallert got into quilting. Caryl is an award-winning artist known for her beautiful, vivid, and expressive art quilts. She says, "An artist is something you are born to be, in my case at least. Artists have a certain way of looking at things and curiosity about things and often look at things from a slightly different point of view than everyone else. All my life I can't remember not drawing or painting, and I've been sewing since I was ten years old. When I discovered I could make art from cloth, that is when I found the medium that best expressed my artistic vision. No one actually warned me that it was addictive! For the images that I'm creating I found quilting to be the most expressive medium."

Quilter and host of HGTV's *Simply Quilts* Alex Anderson tells a similar story. "I have always been intrigued with sewing and fiber arts since a very young age. In college I thought I was going to be a weaver for life (it was an acceptable form of art)—however, when I saw a quilt show in Oakland, I realized that quilting could be viewed as art and at that moment I was hooked for life."

Journal quilts are a type of art quilt that tell a story. They often consist of several blocks or panels that depict an event or situation in the maker's life. Journal quilts can be any size and they use whatever techniques are necessary to illustrate the story. Some artists use journal quilts to depict a struggle with illness or the loss of a loved one. Some of them reflect the artist's love of nature or a favorite pet or family member. Quilt shows often have journal quilt displays where artists answer a challenge— like creating a journal block for each month in order to visually document a year of one's life. These quilts can provide an interesting glimpse into the life of the artist and a vivid representation of his or her feelings on a variety of subjects.

Quilted **postcards** and trading cards can also be considered art quilts. They have gained popularity in recent years and are often made by quilters as fun gifts or to trade with other quilters. They are often quite personal and, like any art quilt, can reflect the values and beliefs of the quilt maker. These items are purely decorative and are made from a variety of materials. They borrow a lot from scrapbooking and use all kinds of found objects, charms, buttons, beads, lace, jewels, feathers, and whatever the artist needs to express his or her thoughts. Quilted postcards are generally made from fabric bonded or glued to a stiff interfacing material. They can be hand cancelled and sent through the normal postal mail, and many online quilt groups swap postcards as a way to get to know one another.

Clothing and Fashion Quilts

In the past, quilts were often made from worn-out, discarded clothing. Nowadays many quilters buy fresh yardage specifically to create quilted clothing.

There are practical as well as artistic reasons to make quilted clothing. Quilted clothing is warm, and many cultures have used it historically for just that reason. Quilted clothing can also be decorated in unlimited ways, making something as simple as a jacket outrageously beautiful. Most large quilt shows feature quilted fashions and give prizes for these interesting and beautiful creations.

Often it is a quilter's passion for fabrics that inspires her to make clothing in the first place. I know that when I see gorgeous batiks in a quilt shop I picture full, flowing skirts and funky sundresses just as often as I picture quilts. Some quilt shops sell rayon batik in addition to cotton batik specifically for use in clothing since it is softer and has a nicer drape. But quilters are drawn to anything with a beautiful color or sheen and use all sorts of fabrics in their wearable art creations.

Any quilter who wants something unique that also signifies her passion for fabrics will eventually make a piece of quilted clothing. Some quilters make several items (jackets, vests, hats, handbags, or totes) and get addicted to the versatile beauty of these pieces. They make wonderful gifts, and the choice of fabric and color can personalize them for any given recipient.

There are entire quilt shows devoted to quilted clothing, and many of these shows present very generous prizes to the winners. The creations are always interesting, although most of them are not outfits you'd wear on a daily basis! Some of them are pretty wild . . . and why not? The whole point of creating art is to free yourself from the petty constraints of the world and create something that speaks to your soul. If you think you would like to show off your own wearable art, visit quilts.com/home/contests and sign up for the next show.

Some quilters have never sewn garments. As quilter Leslie Organ writes, "When I was finally ready to try making my first art garment, I chose to start with a simple sweatshirt covered with stitch and flip strips. I selected a number of navy and white recycled garments and cut one-, two-, three-, and five-inch strips from them, which I then seamed together and cut again cross-wise. I ended up with strips that covered a space of about three by six feet. I decided they would make a fine wall hanging. But once they were pinned up on my design wall, I began to envision them as a lined, quilted vest and proceeded to laboriously and painstakingly create it without benefit of a pattern. This project proved to me that, despite my fears, I really could sew garments."

Home Accessory Quilts

Many home accessories can be quilted, including table runners, placemats, curtains, wall hangings, and pillows. They make excellent projects for a new quilter—they're small and offer almost immediate gratification. They can also be used to practice techniques and try out experimental methods that you might not want to try on a large piece.

While you can easily buy quilted home accessories, making your own allows you to be creative and also achieve exactly the look you want. You can easily coordinate a whole room or house by making the accessories yourself. They also make wonderful gifts.

Quilts with a Purpose

Many quilts are designed for specific purposes. Some of these quilts serve as memorials; others are auctioned or displayed to raise money for a cause or to help a certain group. When a quilter participates in making a memorial or charity quilt, he or she is giving time, materials, and creative energy to support the cause.

People who have been directly affected by a tragic event, illness, or misfortune often find that creating the quilt or quilt blocks helps ease their pain. Quilt making is a very personal way to memorialize a loved one, and the practice of going through the familiar motions while thinking fondly of that person (or of the stranger who will be helped by your creation) gives a quilter a deep sense of purpose.

One of the most famous memorial quilts is the Names Project AIDS Memorial Quilt. It was started in 1987 by Cleve Jones; a group of volunteers and quilters from around the world has been adding to it ever since. Each block is in memory of someone who has died of the disease.

According to the aidsquilt.org website, there are more than 46,000 panels on the quilt and more than 91,000 names recorded. The quilt is shown (normally in pieces because of its enormous size, which is currently about 1,293,300 square feet) at fund-raisers and events designed to raise awareness of the illness.

This quilt has even found a home in the virtual world "Second Life," where in June 2007 it was recreated to celebrate Pride Month. The virtual quilt took up several private islands in the three-dimensional world.

The AIDS quilt is not unique among quilts (except perhaps for its sheer size). Several memorial quilts were created after September 11, 2001. These include the WTC Quilt and the 9/11 Memorial Quilt. After Hurricane Katrina, thousands of quilters around the world made quilts to donate to the survivors and to be auctioned off to raise money.

I was one of them.

I read in *American Quilter* magazine that people were collecting quilts, especially baby quilts, for survivors who were suddenly homeless. I looked through my books for just the right pattern and I found one called Bright Hopes. This is a simple square-in-a-square block. For the centers, I chose bright, cheerful prints I'd been given by a friend. Around that square I put a dark brown fabric. Normally the block is just two colors, but my blocks were too small to make anything, and I had run out of the brown fabric. So I decided to add more borders, a bright sunny yellow on half the blocks, and assorted blues on the other half. Finally they were big enough to piece together into a quilt.

As I worked on the quilt, I listened to the news reports of the hurricane and many times wet the fabric with my tears as I heard story after story of people who could not be rescued and died in their attics, and of helpless animals abandoned by panicked owners, left to starve and drown as the waters continued to rise day after day.

After I had the blocks all completed I realized what I had created: out of the blue water and the dark brown mud left by the hurricane, the brilliant yellow sun would come out, and the bright, cheerful flowers would grow again.

I was very pleased with this little quilt and planned to donate it. But time slipped by as I worked on it and as I tried (in vain) to finish quilting it, and by the time it was done, the deadline for donations had passed. It is still in my stash of unfinished work and one day I will complete the quilt and donate it to some other baby who needs some bright hopes.

Quilters are widely known for their generosity, and some quilters do nothing but make charity quilts. This kind of selfless activity serves two purposes: it helps those in need, and it gives the quilter a sense that he or she is helping, in some small way, to make the world a better, more comfortable place for someone in distress.

Charity quilts are often made en masse by quilt bees or guilds and donated to local police or fire departments, to neonatal units of hospitals, to homeless shelters, to disabled war veterans, or to auctions that raise money for charities.

> A guild is defined by Merriam-Webster as "an association of people with similar interests or pursuits." A quilt guild is a group of quilters who meet periodically to discuss quilt-related topics and to share their knowledge with one another. Guilds are generally larger than bees (they can have hundreds of members) and the main activity at their meetings is typically listening to a lecture on a given quilting topic and socializing with other quilters. Guilds often sponsor quilt shows and charity quilt-making efforts so that their members can share their quilts with the community.

Members of the guild to which I belong, Berrien Towne and Country Quilters, recently began making quilts for a local charity called Well of GRACE (Girls Restored and Christ Exalted). This organization provides a safe place for teenage girls to stay when they are experiencing chaos in their lives. One girl wrote the following heartfelt letter to our guild in thanks for a quilt she had received:

Dear Quilting Ladies,

There really are NO words to describe just how grateful I am for having a quilt made just for me. All of your hard work, dedication, and love sure flows through each and every patch and stitch.

When I was told that I could choose a quilt to have as my very own, I was in complete awe. I didn't feel like I was deserving of such a thing after I have hurt myself and refused to let love in. Once I entered Well of GRACE and saw the quilt that I had picked on my bed, I knew it was really mine.

For so long, I have had things given to me, only for them to be taken away because my feelings didn't matter. To have you ladies piece together a quilt that I can call my very own, and to know that it won't be taken or given away truly means the world to me. It's like you all know my favorite color and my style and I know that all the other quilts that have yet to be made will also have other girls feeling just as special and loved as I do.

So I just want to thank each and every one of you for any time you spend on making a quilt, and for all the love that you put into it. You will never know all of the warmth, comfort, and the fears that will be taken away by your love and generosity in making quilts for hurting young women like myself."

M'Liss Rae Hawley tells me that, to her, sharing the items you quilt is like coming full circle in the process of creation. She points out that the quilter goes through all the steps of making the quilt, from selecting or designing the pattern, choosing the fabric, washing it, cutting it, piecing it together, layering, quilting, embellishing and embroidering it—and then gives it away. All the steps of creating the quilt are "self satisfying" steps—we do them because we love to buy and fondle fabric, we love to design quilts, we love to piece them, and some people even love the process of quilting them.

But the very last step, which makes a quilt complete, is giving it away—sharing all the creative energy with the recipient. I've given away most of the quilts I've finished and keep very few for myself. I always take a picture of my quilt, because I know I may never see it again, and if you are giving the quilt to strangers (as when guilds give away hundreds of baby quilts or quilts for charity) the quilter usually loses all track of that work of art . . . that piece of her soul. It goes off into the world and shares the quilter's love and dedication with its eventual owner.

Each quilt, especially one that you designed yourself or even one made from a commercial pattern modified in some way to be your own, contains a part of you. Your choices of color and fabrics, as well as your workmanship, make each quilt special. It can be hard to part with a quilt sometimes, especially if it has deep meaning for you. Some winners of the American Quilter's Society (AQS) Show have been known to refuse the prize money because they did not want to surrender their quilt to the AQS museum. (I'd have to love my quilt a *lot* to refuse ten thousand dollars in prize money! But having seen some of the first-place winners up close and in person, I can fully understand why their creators found it hard to let go.)

Some quilters don't feel this sense of attachment. To them, the creative process is more important than the quilt itself. Caryl Bryer Fallert acknowledges this when she says, "The great adventure of quilting is having the idea and going through the creative journey. When the quilt is finished, it's just stuff. I hope it will go find a home for itself, like adult children do. It is all about making the quilt; it is not about having the finished project."

For many people, knowing that their quilt has found a home where it is loved and cherished is reward enough for all their time and effort. The West Michigan Quilters' Guild, to which I used to belong, typically donates about four hundred baby quilts to the neonatal unit at the local hospital every Christmas. Many of these quilts are wrapped around dolls and stuffed animals. The parents of premature newborns choose from among dozens of lovingly handmade quilts in which to take their baby home. None of the guild members *has* to do this, and they all have their own projects to work on, but each year many of them make multiple quilts to donate just so they will have the experience of sharing their love and creativity with others.

M'Liss says that giving quilts to those who are ill (or to orphans or others in misfortune) is like giving them hope. To her, making the quilt is joy, but sharing it with the world is even better.

In addition to local groups, there are many national groups that coordinate the donation of quilts. One of the best known is Project Linus (named after the *Peanuts* character), a nonprofit volunteer organization. According to its website, its mission is "to provide love, a sense of security, warmth, and comfort to children who are seriously ill, traumatized, or otherwise in need through the gifts of new, handmade blankets and afghans, lovingly created by volunteer 'blanketeers' . . . to provide a rewarding and fun service opportunity for interested individuals and groups in local communities, for the benefit of children." As of September 2007, Project Linus had donated 2,293,340 blankets and quilts!

My friend Joyce DenBleyker has made quilts for Project Linus. She is teaching her daughter and stepchildren how to quilt and each of them has participated in making a quilt for the charity. The kids chose the fabrics and Joyce did most of the finishing work. I think this is a great way to not only pass on the love of quilting, but also to get young people involved in good causes and let them see that helping the less fortunate does not have to be a chore, but can actually be a fun experience.

Quilts for Kids is another nonprofit group that collects quilts (as well as quilting fabrics and supplies) and "transforms discontinued designer fabrics into quilts that comfort children with cancer, AIDS, and other life-threatening illnesses as well as battered and abused children." Their goal is to "link design centers nationwide to their communities, so that children in need in those regions may be served."

Most quilters are women, and many have either been stricken with breast cancer or know someone who has. When a friend tells you she has found a lump, all you can do is wish her well and hope that it is something minor that can be cured with surgery and therapy. It's a helpless feeling, because nothing you can do will make her situation any better. All you can do is be a friend and be there for her. But quilters can help find a cure for breast cancer by participating in Quilt Pink.

Quilt Pink is a charity quilt auction sponsored by *American Patchwork and Quilting* magazine, Moda Fabrics, Husqvarna Viking, AccuCut, and Handi Quilter. In May 2007 the organization auctioned off more than four thousand quilts, with proceeds going to Susan G. Komen for the Cure, a foundation established in 1982 by Nancy Brinker to honor the memory of her sister who died of breast cancer at the age of thirty-six. Quilt Pink is an annual event; every September, quilt shops around the world sponsor Quilt Pink stitch-ins where quilters make blocks that are sewn together to make the auction quilts. Many of the quilts feature pink fabrics and the familiar pink ribbon symbol. Many quilt supply manufacturers also make pink cutting mats, rotary cutters, and other quilting notions with part of the proceeds from the sale of these items going to the Quilt for a Cure charity.

Quilts of Valor is a group dedicated to making quilts for members of the armed forces. Many guilds collect fabric and blocks and donate quilts, including lap quilts for veterans who are restricted to wheelchairs. Individuals can also take part. My fellow guild member Cindy Shepherd says, "I love to quilt for a good cause. Quilting for Quilts of Valor is a way of expressing my sincere thank-you for their service and giving us the freedom to quilt whenever we want to . . . I find it important to share the items we make from the talents God has given us. After all, aren't we here to blanket each other in warmth and love? Some of us just do it with quilts!"

Quilts with Unconscious Meaning

Sometimes I'll sit back and say, "Wow, that's inspired! Look what I did with those fabrics!"

—M'LISS RAE HAWLEY

The style of the quilt can sometimes be used as another means by which the quilter expresses his or her emotions; but, really, any kind of quilt can convey the thoughts and feelings of the quilter if she takes some time to decide how to express them. Sometimes the real meaning behind the quilt is not apparent— even to the quilter—until the quilt is completed.

Caryl Bryer Fallert tells me how she had made a quilt almost by accident after a very trying time. Her mother had recently passed away and her husband had almost died of a stroke. She had won best of show at the American Quilter's Society Show in Paducah, Kentucky, had written her first book, and had a traveling exhibition—all at the same time. On the last day of the year she went to her studio at seven in the morning to clear up paperwork, and found an address label with a little bird on it. She liked the design and decided to scan it before throwing the label away. But something about the little bird intrigued her. She started to doodle and put things together . . . and twelve hours later had used the bird motif to create a quilt.

As she worked on it, she began to see human forms in the quilt, so she added faces. She ended up with two faces looking in opposite directions with the bird between them. Caryl often includes birds in her quilts when the theme is healing or spirituality. She saw the bird in this quilt as a messenger of hope for a new beginning after a trying roller coaster of a year.

Her quilt, Messenger #2, came straight out of her unconscious mind with no conscious thought of what it was about. The meaning of the quilt only came out after several hours of working on it.

Milestone Quilts

Milestones in life are usually marked with celebrations and often with gifts. Most quilters have made quilts to mark milestones in the lives of their loved ones. Wedding quilts were traditionally made by the prospective bride herself, as part of her hope chest. In earlier days when nearly every girl was taught needlework, making your own wedding quilt was expected of you. These quilts often featured exquisite workmanship and, because they were special, they were rarely used and were handed down through generations. Many of the antique quilts in collections today were originally wedding quilts because the everyday quilts were worn out from use and did not survive.

Many grandmothers and even expectant moms and dads make baby quilts in anticipation of a birth. These quilts run the gamut from frilly pastel confections to bright and cheerful crib quilts or wall hangings. Birthdays, graduations, anniversaries, and retirements are often marked by a memory quilt. Modern memory quilts use computer technology to print photographs or letters directly on fabric. These digital artifacts are then sewn into the quilt top. Graduation quilts often feature blocks made from T-shirts and sweatshirts owned by the recipient. They make wonderful mementos of one's school years by incorporating the individual's interests directly into the quilt.

Even milestones such as retirement can inspire quilts. Farewell to the Silver Bird is a quilt made by Caryl Bryer Fallert when she retired from United Airlines after twenty-eight years as a flight attendant. On her website, Caryl says, "This quilt represents my taking leave of the corporation to fly solo in my own career. The silver bird, naturally, represents the airline. The globe represents the areas where I flew professionally in my twenty-eight-year career: from Alaska to Venezuela and from Montreal to Hawaii. The red, orange, and blue stripes in the border are the logo stripes found on every United airplane. The bird flying away is made from the spectral colors of light that I often use in my quilts to represent life and energy."

Spiritual Quilts

> . . . expressing my creativity provides a way for me
> to mirror the creative activity of the divine.
> —BETH ANN WILLIAMS

There are many books devoted to spirituality and quilting. Some are devotional texts that provide prayers and meditations for the quilter to contemplate while working on a quilt, while others feature quilt block designs with a spiritual theme. But one can combine quilting and spirituality in other ways. An interested quilter could use themes from a religious conference or sermon to design a banner or wall hanging for his or her sacred meeting place, or use religious symbols from history or other cultures such as mandalas and labyrinths to express her spirituality in quilt form.

My fellow bee member Phyllis Jackson is a retired school-teacher. She is married to a church minister and is active in a number of church groups for which she makes banners.

Recently she made a banner based on a conference theme of

> Quilt bees are groups of people who come together periodically to sew and quilt. They may all work on the same quilt, or each member may work on his or her own project. A quilt bee can mean the members of such a group collectively, or it can mean an old-fashioned quilting bee, which is a group that comes together for the purpose of completing one or more quilts, usually all working on the same quilt at the same time.

Resurrection Women. The theme was intended to celebrate the women who discovered that Jesus had risen from the tomb, but Phyllis thought a tomb would be too depressing to put on a quilt. After some thought, she decided to feature butterflies in the piece. They emerge from the cocoon in a blaze of color and fly off into the sky, and Phyllis saw it as a great metaphor for the resurrection of Jesus. She created a delightful pieced and appliquéd wall hanging that depicts two women, arms outstretched, releasing a bevy of colorful butterflies.

She says, "It's always a great honor for me to be asked to create a quilted banner for a specific theme or occasion. It means that I really need to dig into my creative talents and come up with something fitting and appropriate. I take great pride in doing this. I feel that God has given me some special talents, and I need to share them with others. At the moment that I present my finished project, I feel so proud and very blessed."

Sally Zehrung agrees. "I believe there is definitely a spiritual side to art. Often what I create is an expression of something meaningful to me. The piece I just finished is called Oregon Rainforest (I'm a native Oregonian). It's very different from other things I've done. It's pictorial. I strove to create the feeling of being in an old-growth forest just after a rain, with the sun just coming out. The wet plants sparkle. It would be an awesome place to be. I was told by one person that she could almost smell the trees. There is a feeling of reverence in a forest like that."

My own attempt at a spiritual quilt was more along the lines of Sally's effort than Phyllis's. My beliefs tend more toward those of a worshipper of nature and the female divine. The result was a (still unfinished) wall hanging. It features a goddess figure, hands upraised to the moon. Her body is in dark purple shadows and the sky is a deep, rich blue with a pale, fat full moon centered between her outstretched hands. I wanted her attitude to be one of sheer joy and wonder, as I always feel when I look up at the moon.

The border (when and if I ever finish it) will feature small Celtic symbols and other sacred shapes on brightly colored backgrounds bordered in black. I gave up on completing the quilt because I didn't like how the head on the figure looked. I may have to try again. I think my moon-worshipping goddess form would feel right at home in Sally's forest!

Quilter Marlene Brown Woodfield creates wall hangings, altar cloths, and pulpit and lectern covers for her church. She says, "I feel that I should tithe with these since it is a gift to be able to create beauty."

Sally and Marlene were both quilters featured at the Sacred Threads show I attended in June of 2007. A group of quilters who made spiritual or sacred quilts joined forces in 1999 and founded the show, which runs biannually near Columbus, Ohio. According to their website, the committee members "wanted to share the experiences of quilters whose stories would be a source of healing and strength for others by allowing the artist to submit a statement that would be exhibited with the artwork that described the meaning or inspiration for the piece . . . The show does not emphasize any particular religion or theology but conveys the spirituality, healing and inspirational messages that transcend all religions and races."

The sheer variety of quilts I saw at the show was astounding, from very simple wall hangings to very elaborate rope bridges made of fibers and textiles, from traditional pieced quilts to wildly imaginative art quilts.

The quilts that struck me the most were those created by people who were grieving the loss of a loved one. Halfway through viewing the grief section, I had to stop and take a break. My fiancé and I walked out into the lobby for a breath of fresh air. One of the ladies at the admission desk asked if we were done already, and I told her we just needed a break from the grief quilts. She said she understood perfectly and offered me a bottle of water and box of tissues. Participating quilters had seen the impact of their quilts on visitors before, and every table and bench had its own box of tissues. These ladies were definitely prepared for the effect their art has on people. The pain poured out in these quilts was stunning, but the amount of healing that the act of putting emotion into art produced was equally stunning.

Grief Quilts

Many quilters create quilts to commemorate deceased friends or relatives, or to help themselves heal from the grief of losing a loved one. Sometimes these quilts are anonymous—kept by the quilter and her family as treasured heirlooms of remembrance. Sometimes the work is so extraordinary that it becomes well known and wins awards.

One such quilt is known as the 1776 quilt. The 1776 quilt's creator, Pam Holland, started it while her twenty-four-year-old daughter was dying from cancer. She says in her book *The 1776*

Quilt: Heartache, Heritage, and Happiness, "It was my therapy as I watched my beautiful daughter struggle with her disease. My emotions were hidden in every stitch." Her labor of love went on to win best-in-show at four major American shows.

Although I have never made a grief quilt, I can see how having something to focus on, something that one has control over, could help when coping with grief. The repetitive nature of cutting, piecing, and stitching a quilt can become meditative and calming and allow you to be "busy" while at the same time letting your brain focus on something besides the pain.

Sometimes grief can only be processed after the fact. At the time of a loved one's death, you are often shocked and dumbstruck, going through the motions that get you through the day, but not able to really sit and sort out all the feelings surging inside of you. This was the case for Mary Beedlow, about whom I read in *Quilter's Home* magazine, when her husband Joe died suddenly in the midst of building their dream home, a log cabin. Mary was left in midwinter with "a house with no roof, no heat, no windows, and no doors." She was also left with two young teenage sons who needed her more than ever.

Together, they finished building the house: they got on with doing what needed to be done, and there was little time for tears or grief. After the house was completed, a woman Mary knew asked her to make her a quilt. At first she was disinclined to take on the task, but then decided to do it anyway. Mary says, "I discovered in pulling out my machine and getting to work that I had found my therapy. While I was piecing, I didn't have to worry about anything else. Once I discovered this breakthrough, other barriers melted."

Mary took on other quilting projects and eventually opened her own home-based business, Orchard's Edge Machine Quilting. Working on these projects for others has helped Mary to grieve and heal. She says, "I'm not quite ready to make a memorial quilt, yet. When I do, the quilt will hang in a private area of our home."

Sally Zerhung wrote to me about a grief quilt she made that was featured in the Sacred Threads show. "I created a quilt while healing . . . from the loss of my brother. That was The Light at the End of the Tunnel, which was at the Sacred Threads exhibit . . . the Tunnel quilt was by far the most meaningful to me. My brother and I had always been close. He was four years older than I. He was always there. He had cancer that was supposedly all removed. Then suddenly it was back. That, along with some other serious health issues, was just too much. His last days were very short. I wasn't able to see him. It broke my heart. So the old saying about the light at the end of the tunnel came to my mind. I knew things wouldn't look so dark and gloomy forever, but at the time I needed to see a little light, so I made the quilt. It's still my favorite one. I call it my therapy quilt."

Angie Crosson says that while creating a quilt for a sick loved one, "I felt like I was saying everything in my heart; get well, you're in my prayers, sorry you're not better, and ultimately, good-bye."

One of the most touching grief quilts I have seen was created by members of my guild for a member who was dying of a very swift-moving cancer. Members traced their hands and appliquéd them to quilt blocks. Antique handkerchiefs were tucked into the hands. When the quilt was shown during show-and-tell, the lady who had organized it cried through the whole presentation. The recipient said that she got her first good night's sleep in months under the quilt. Instead of flowers, she wants the quilt to cover her casket and she wants the quilt tucked around her when she is buried. Our usually boisterous group was in tears. It is events like this that makes you know that your quilting has some meaning beyond mere necessity.

Recovery Quilts

Quilting as therapy is a theme I heard over and over again as I spoke to quilters about why they quilt. One quilter, Debbie Krueger, actually titled her quilt My Therapy Quilt.

Debbie says, "My Therapy Quilt definitely helped me to heal. Though the story is long, I'll share it here. I love the pattern Grandmother's Flower Garden. It's probably the only traditional pattern that I willingly choose to make. I had a beautiful batik fabric that I was going to make into this pattern. I had taken care of my mother for a long time, and after her death I suffered from the 'What do I do now?' syndrome.

"One night, in the middle of a bout of tears, I started laying the hexagons on the living room floor, wondering if I could make little question marks rather than flowers. One thing led to another and the little question marks became a huge one symbolic of my mind screaming, 'Why do I exist?' and I decided the question mark would be the centerpiece of my quilt. I decided to put a lot of small question marks around the big one.

"In the midst of this, I moved out of my childhood house and into an apartment and started looking at my life in a new way. One day, as I started to lay out the question marks, I thought they looked like the petals of flowers. The flowers became the symbol of my growth even though there were still questions. I purposely made the stems of the flowers free form, which for me was a departure from the anal-retentive methods I would have used in the past! For the first time I allowed the quilt to speak to me and it nearly designed itself."

Physical illness can also hamper creativity. Another Sacred Threads artist, JoAnn Perkins, writes that she was in a creative slump while recovering from breast cancer. She just could not get motivated to do anything. Then one day she walked into a quilt shop and "the perfect" fabric was staring her in the face. (This happens to me all the time; hence my enormous stash . . .)

JoAnn used this perfect fabric to create a bargello quilt, a style she had long wanted to learn. She writes, "Just as the bargello design is made up of many small pieces with fluctuating highs and lows and darks and lights, so was my life affected by moments of darkness, but faith, family, and friends were there to support and lift my spirit. I wanted to show that even though it was a difficult time for me and there were many highs and lows and moments of darkness, there was much positive energy and goodness during that time as well. And it can be that way for anyone, should they choose that path."

> Bargello is a sharply pointed pattern that resembles flames. It can also be modified into graceful curves and other designs. The name comes from the Bargello Palace in Florence, which had furnishings featuring needlework in this pattern. Quilted bargello patterns use strategically placed pieces of fabric to mimic the look of bargello stitching.

My friend Beth Ann Williams says, "Quilt making has also been an important factor in allowing me to define my own identity. Any chronic, debilitating disease such as multiple sclerosis potentially has the power to dominate one's sense of self, or control how one is perceived in the world. Developing my creative self, in large part through my quilt making, has given me a wonderful arena in which I can feel whole and free."

She adds, "I don't struggle with loss of motivation so much as I do loss of physical capabilities. Diseases like multiple sclerosis can be quite capricious. You never know from day to day what your body will do. It takes concentration to focus on accepting each 'good' day for the grace that it is, and not drowning in an abyss of despair and fear during the 'bad' days, weeks, or months.

"I know that when I'm ill, quilting is the last thing I want to do! I just don't have the energy to stand and cut fabric or sit and sew at a time like that. But if I'm laid up in bed and have run out of books to read, I do love to doodle new quilt designs. I keep graph paper and colored pencils in my nightstand to capture late-night inspirations. My pencil sketches out patterns I will probably never have the skills to master. But thinking up the designs is the best part for me, even if they never turn into creations of fabric and thread."

So if you are ever in a place where you can't sew or are too ill to handle the physical aspects of quilting, you can always fall back on designing your next masterpiece on paper. You might even turn your doodles into commercial patterns and a whole new career could be born!

Quilts of Joy and Love

Other quilts in the Sacred Threads show represent joy and love. Debbie Krueger created a quilt based on love letters between her parents. "When my brother and I were cleaning out my parents' house after my mom's death, we found a box of love letters my dad had written to my mother over about two years, when they were in college and while they were engaged," Debbie explains. "After I moved and had some time, I spent a day putting the letters in order by date and reading them. What you have to understand is that though Mom always talked about her love for my dad, I had never really heard Dad talk about his love for Mom."

She continues, "The letters were filled with wonderful insight to my parents' youth and how much my dad loved my mother. I also learned that they were very human (something we never credit our parents with)—including pregnancy scares (contrary to the 'don't do anything 'til you're married' teachings of my mom) and hopes and dreams for their future (my favorite comment is when my dad says that even if they someday have a daughter, she will never have the 'old man' feel about her the way he did about Mom). Somewhere in the midst of the reading session, I knew a quilt was in the making."

And that quilt became special. "So this new knowledge of my parents' love gave me such a feeling of comfort and joy that the quilt became an expression of my love for them. Filled with photos of them during their courtship days, their wedding, and their twenty-fifth anniversary as well as portions of the letters, the quilt has yellow silk roses (my dad's fraternity flower which he always gave my mother on special occasions) and their fraternity and sorority pins in a gold heart (gold to symbolize that this year would have been their fiftieth anniversary). I named the quilt All My Love, Doug, because I never knew Dad to sign his letters, cards, flower cards—anything, really—in any other way than 'All my love, Doug.' It's a small quilt, but the love and joy behind it are huge!"

Let this be a lesson! Be careful what you leave lying around—your children might one day share it with the whole world! Quilters find inspiration in all sorts of places. If Debbie were a writer, or a poet, or a lyricist, these love letters may have found expression in some other form. This just shows that quilters can take inspiration from the same sources as any other artist. If you are stuck for an idea, look around. Not only nature and current events, but family history can provide a creative spark that will make your quilts even more meaningful to your heirs as they will contain a piece of their own past.

Cindy Shepherd writes that "every quilt I make is a celebration that I lived another day to complete the project. When I look at the quilts I made, some make me laugh, some bring back memories of the vacation that inspired me or that I took it with to work on. Some bring me joy because I can't believe I won a ribbon on it. I am thankful for some quilts because God gave me the knowledge and strength to finish the project. Whew, some patterns are doozies!"

Quilts That are Meant to Be

Sometimes a quilt just evolves from a series of seemingly random ideas. You'll be quilting along and all of a sudden some little detail hits you—it could be from a song or a book you're reading, something someone says, or something you see on TV. Some little idea will ignite a spark and then another and another and before you know it, you have incorporated all these disparate elements into your quilt.

Roslyn Besterman relates a story of how a trail of serendipitous events helped her design her quilt Order out of Chaos. It all started when Roslyn won a drawing for patriotic fabrics at a guild meeting in June 2002. Although she was very busy she says she felt compelled to design a quilt, maybe for Flag Day or Fourth of July. Circumstances seemed to be against her from the start though.

She envisioned a flag fluttering in the wind so she started with a tessellating pattern but the pieces on her design wall were chaotic, not fluttering. She felt a little down because the quilt was not turning out as planned and almost stopped right there. But when she ran out of red fabric and found that her local quilt shop only had one yard left she took it as a sign that she should finish her quilt now, so she bought the red and continued on.

In August, her guild mates showed off their flag and patriotic-themed quilts, but hers was not ready for prime time. Even when they announced that the following month's meeting would take place on September 11, Roslyn says, "It still didn't hit me."

While assembling the border, Roslyn tried again to achieve that elusive fluttering look, using scraps given her by a friend. But it didn't look right until she had bordered her tessellated flag with a tidy border of smaller flags. She says, "It hit me right in the face. Order out of Chaos. This flag was meant for September 11."

Some suggestions from friends in her quilt group led to a red border with white cornerstones. Roslyn decided on red stars: red for blood and the four planes. While looking for the name of the pattern she had used, Roslyn realized it was called propellers, so she quilted a propeller design in the white spaces. The propellers reminded Roslyn of a dream she'd had of spider-like creatures with hundreds of legs spinning on the floor. Someone in her dream called them anacondas, which made no sense to her at the time. Later she heard a newscast that showed helicopters spinning around in Afghanistan. They were calling it Operation Anaconda.

All these disparate events seemed to be conspiring to become part of Roslyn's quilt. On September 11, 2002, Roslyn heard the mayor of New York use the phrase, "order out of chaos," and she knew then that her quilt wanted and needed to be completed for September 11, and it was.

This kind of synchronicity may seem rare and random, but when you are open to the universe surprising things can happen. Roslyn's heart was open enough to see the little signs and coincidences and somehow they all converged to create this quilt that perfectly expressed her feelings about the events of September 11.

TWO

Quilting as a Career

Art is making something out of nothing and selling it.
—Frank Zappa

To truly open your heart and be in touch with the world in a tangible way, it helps if you can do what you love as often as possible. You may think you don't have the time to quilt. It's true, that quilting takes time and energy, a dedicated space, and a certain amount of peace and quiet (or at least solitude). But if these things are lacking in your life, you can still make time to quilt.

Our forebearers sewed by hand, working on blocks or small pieces whenever they had a chance to sit down and pick up a needle. I know many quilters who carry blocks to hand stitch while waiting for appointments, while traveling on the bus, or while riding in the car or RV with their spouse. By fitting in a little sewing here and there these women are able to make more quilts than I'll ever be able to make with my sewing machine. And they have the added pleasure of perfecting their hand stitching and doing what they love almost any time, any place.

Another way to do what you love more often is to make it

your life's work. Some people trudge through life, working at a thankless job, doing what they have to do to get by financially, while harboring a secret desire to strike out on their own and do something they truly love. Some of us are lucky enough to have enough money and leisure time to follow our passion in our spare time, and that may be the best we can achieve—at least for now. But others have reached career nirvana: they are actually working at what they love every day!

I spoke to several quilters who have been courageous and lucky enough to turn their passion into a thriving career. Each of them works full or part time in the quilt industry. They have the best of both worlds—doing what they love, and making money at it! While it is definitely still hard work to be your own boss, it beats the alternative by a mile!

Everyone has to start somewhere, and sometimes the most unlikely people become famous for their innovative techniques or creative designs. Eleanor Burns is a well-known quilter who started her Quilt in a Day business while raising two small boys. Being a busy mom, she had to develop speed-piecing techniques, and she popularized strip piecing, the process of cutting long strips of fabric, piecing them together, then cutting them crossways to create checkerboard and other patterns. She self-published her first book and began teaching classes. After her marriage ended, she used her love of quilting to support herself and her children. She now has a line of more than seventy *Quilt in a Day* books, a sewing machine named after her (the Elna, which I own), her own fabric lines, and a shop in Paducah, Kentucky. Her son Orion even helps out at the shop and at quilt shows all over the country! Eleanor is just one of many individuals who have taken their passion for quilting and turned it into a livelihood. If you have a bright and original idea, you could too!

Custom Piecing

When people think of making a living as a quilter, they often think first of people who make quilts for sale. This is usually the easiest way to get started in the quilting industry if your goal is to earn some money; however, many people do not see the value in a quilt and expect a custom-designed, handmade quilt to cost the same as a mass-produced quilted bedcover sold in a discount store. That is unfortunate; it completely devalues the real worth of a custom quilt. The quilter often has to educate his or her customers to make them realize that what they are getting is a unique piece of art, not just an off-the-shelf consumer item.

When you consider all the expenses that a quilt maker has, you realize that people who sell their quilts at county fairs and other similar venues for fifty or one hundred dollars are selling themselves way short! Consider the normal expenses of a self-employed person—in addition to your valuable time, you are giving the customer your design expertise, sewing expertise, and all of the materials required to create the quilt. This is where most people stop figuring. But if you are going to quilt for others as a career you need to factor in things like hardware (pins, needles, sewing machine, rulers, cutting mats, rotary cutters, and other tools of the trade) and the wear and tear on that hardware. You also have to figure in utilities for your home or studio, the cost of your website, e-mail address, telephone, and other advertising and communication methods. Then you have to count necessities like health insurance, income tax, tax preparation related to your business, and a whole host of other expenses. How could you pay for all that out of the sale of a fifty-dollar quilt?

One way to ensure that people value the time, effort, and talent you put into a quilt is to find a niche—some specialization that will make people realize right off the bat that your quilt is a unique item and worth the money you charge. This can be done by quilting to a particular audience.

Custom Quilt Maker Boo Davis

While I was writing this book, an acquaintance of mine pointed me to the website of a quilter who specializes in heavy-metal quilts. No, her quilts are not made from steel—they feature images, words, and themes associated with heavy-metal music. The owner of Quiltsrÿche, Boo Davis, charges what I consider to be a reasonable price for her one-of-a-kind "metalhead" quilts, some of which cost thousands of dollars. She can do this because her market is very focused on one particular type of consumer who is looking for a very special kind of quilt. They will never find a quilt like this at the local discount store!

The advantage to making custom quilts in this way is that you get to do what you love (create quilts on a specific theme or style) and get paid a decent amount for doing so by people who will love and appreciate your work. I asked Boo to talk about her unique quilts and the business of making niche quilts.

"I haven't exactly cracked the code of a business model that would allow me to quilt full time," she laughs. "My day job is doing design and illustration for a daily newspaper, where I've been employed the past eight years. I'm finding that while many people love the idea of heavy-metal quilts, they're not exactly beating down my door to buy one. And I'm fine with that. I don't want to live in a sweatshop! Right now my approach is to produce a handful of quilts each year—quilts that I make to please just myself—and submit them to art shows and other exhibitions. If someone is willing to shell out the dough for a custom quilt that will suck away a few months of my life, I'll certainly consider it. But I put my heart and soul and hundreds of hours into a quilt, and I don't part with them easily."

She continues, "Each quilt's color and pattern configuration is like a code to be cracked. In the piles of fabrics there exists a quilt, and it's my job to sort it out. Today everything is over designed and focus-group tested to the point where everything is so attractive and predictable. Just give me something hideous! I want questionable color combinations and terrible floral patterns that make me cringe a little. I want crooked seams and misaligned pieces. And that's what I aim for: quilts that are exquisite in their imperfection. I want to make heirloom-quality pieces that could have been made by your half-blind, Metallica-loving grandma—who loves you very, very much."

Boo's quilts echo other quilts such as those of the ladies of Gee's Bend. They too used wild patterns, asymmetrical design, and a seemingly random placement of elements that evoke a naive beauty. Boo's quilt Instrumental, if it didn't have the giant lettering on it, is very reminiscent of their style.

"I began with hand-piecing quilts in college, and then graduated to a sewing machine to streamline the production of baby quilts I was making for expectant friends. Once I was secure in my quilting skills, I was able to approach quilt making differently. I just asked myself, 'What is meaningful to me? What would I want to hand down to my grandkids?' That's when Quiltsrÿche was born. It was just obvious I needed to make heavy-metal quilts. Reinterpreting simple traditional quilt designs in a metal way—that juxtaposition makes me giddy. Cute and evil have always been at the heart of everything I love."

I asked Boo how her customers find her. "Honestly, I haven't done anything in the way of promotion except launch a website. I've been incredibly lucky to get some attention on a few blogs—and things have taken off from there in some ways."

So if any of you have a hankering for a heavy-metal quilt or have a child or grandchild who'd love one, look up Boo's website at quiltsryche.com. Her Primer quilt might be the perfect thing for the little metalhead in your life!

Custom Quilting

Another aspect of custom quilting is doing the actual quilting on other people's quilt tops. I have dozens of quilt tops I've made over the years, and almost none of them get quilted unless someone wants to buy one or I have to finish it to give as a gift. I do not enjoy the process of quilting the layers together. To me the challenge and the fun come from designing the quilt top, choosing the fabrics and piecing the top together like a jigsaw puzzle. Once I have seen how the top looks, I tend to lose interest and the piece never gets quilted. (Thus, I have a large collection of UFOs—UnFinished Objects!) Luckily, there are people out there who *love* to finish quilts! They pay tens of thousands of dollars for giant longarm quilt machines and then charge people a fee for completing the quilting.

Getting started as a longarm quilter takes a large initial investment. The machines (called longarms because the arm of the machine is much longer than a standard household machine) are costly. Then the quilter still has to invest time in learning to use it and practicing until he or she is good enough to quilt other people's quilt tops. Good longarm machine quilters are always in demand and their prices vary based on their experience, quality of their work, and how busy they may be in a given season.

If you are interested in longarm quilting you can usually try out a machine at a large quilt show. Some shops also have them in stock and allow customers to play with them. There are classes you can take so that you are not learning completely on your own. Some are offered by places like longarmuniversity.com.

Owning a Quilt Shop

It has been my dream since about 1999 to own my own quilt shop. I have a business plan written, a floor plan drawn up, a name chosen, an employee handbook written, a list of all the kinds of stock I would carry. I have everything except the building itself and the means to open it! Whenever my day job gets boring, I turn back to that business plan, refining and updating it, daydreaming over the "someday" when I can have my own shop and be my own boss.

I imagine me and my best friend, Laura, running the shop, going on buying trips to the big shows in Houston and Chicago, stocking the shelves, teaching classes, making samples, and helping new quilters discover the joy of making something beautiful and original out of nothing more than cloth and thread.

Writing this book gave me a perfect opportunity to find out if my dreams are anywhere close to reality. I interviewed quilt shop owner Sharon Jager, who owns Sharon's Quilts and More in Allegan, Michigan. Allegan is a small town of about five thousand people. It does not have much industry, but it does attract summer tourists with its proximity to the beautiful beaches of Lake Michigan. Sharon opened her shop in 2005.

Quilt Shop Owner Sharon Jager

Why did you open a quilt shop?

I opened up a quilt shop for a variety of reasons. I love fabric. There are so many beautiful fabrics to choose from today. And I love to sew. Quilting, unlike making an outfit, can take you anywhere. You can make a utility quilt to keep someone warm or you can create a work of art, or anything in-between. I also was thinking of my retirement. Social Security is not enough to retire on and our investments have been slow to recover from the ups and downs. I am also the type of person that cannot sit around the house all day. I have always worked and will continue to do so. I wanted to do something I absolutely love, so I opened up a store. This way I can spread my enthusiasm for this wonderful form of art. It is something everyone can do if they choose to try.

What is the most important trait a quilt shop owner has to have?

The most important trait that a quilt shop owner has to have is a love of quilting and the desire to inspire others to quilt.

How do you see yourself in relation to your customers?

My customers are all very special to me. Each one brings a certain joy and personality into the store. I not only guide and teach my customers, I also listen. There is much to be learned. When someone comes in and says I could never learn to do that, I try to encourage them by maybe suggesting something smaller and less daunting such as a fast-2-fuse project (a box or bowl) or maybe a potholder or placemat. One intangible thing I offer my customers is my attention. (Quilters/sewers love to talk about their projects. Some even bring in their projects to show me.) These are the best of times. I also give advice and pointers. Each quilt that is brought in, no matter the level of skill, is beautiful. There is always something great about each quilt. Whether it be color, or fabric choices, or exceptional sewing skills.

Quilting is a way of expressing yourself. It can tell a story or just give pleasure to someone. Quilting can also be very calming and relaxing. I have taught children with ADHD who will sit for hours and quilt but cannot watch their favorite cartoon for more than thirty seconds. When a quilt is completed, there is a great satisfaction of having created a thing of beauty and comfort.

Quilting has a history of many great stories told down through the centuries. I just put a label on a quilt for one of my customers that stated Grandmother made the quilt in 1923 and gave it to her daughter for her wedding in 1946, she in turn gave it to her daughter as a wedding present in 1974 and *she* in turn gave it to her niece in 2007 because she had no children. I had made a quilt for my mother. I put in it all of the things she loved, birds and flowers, and pictures of all nine of her children. I also have donated a couple of quilts to Safe Harbor to benefit children. Children are our greatest joy and to help one child can give a person a great deal of joy and satisfaction.

Can you tell me about any particular quilt you have made that helped you feel closer to others in some way?

As the only fabric store in town, I was asked to head up a project wherein people would volunteer to make banners to be hung up for the Fourth of July honoring our military heroes (from Allegan) serving today. The Arts Council brought in a picture of what they wanted and I made the pattern and got people to sign up. I volunteered our classroom, some of the materials, and my time, and showed the volunteers how to make the banners. They ended up beautiful and hung up in the city for the month of July. Some of the colors faded with the hot sun but none of the pride and joy faded in those who helped. A lot of compliments were received by all.

Designing Quilt Patterns

I love to doodle quilt patterns on paper, or with software such as Electric Quilt. Some of these creations find their way onto my design wall and under my needle, but often they remain on paper or on screen. Some people turn quilt pattern design into their main career, or us it as an offshoot of an existing quilt-related career.

M'Liss Rae Hawley writes books featuring her own quilt patterns and techniques. M'Liss said that she feels very passionate about sharing her quilting (she sees it as a "gift from God") so when she is at home in her studio she is sharing her gift by designing quilts that other people can make. Unlike art quilts, which are one-of-a-kind and can't really be duplicated, M'Liss enjoys knowing that others can use her patterns, and so she tries to make them easy to follow so that quilters of any skill level can make them and share the joy of the process of making the quilt. She hopes that they can experience the "essence of quilting" when making her quilts.

I asked M'Liss if she ever just got completely lost in the fun and joy of playing with her fabric and produced something totally unexpected.

She says, "Pretty much always!" She has a vague plan before she starts because the patterns will be published and have to be easily duplicated. They also have to fit within the "rules" of the book she is writing. For example, if the book is about "fat quarters" or "scrappy" quilts, then that theme is in the back of her mind as she plans the patterns.

M'Liss reduces her variables to the limits of the publication; however, she is open to changing her mind and is often surprised by what happens during the design process. Sometimes she sits back and says "Wow, that's inspired! Look what I did with those fabrics!"

She says that this kind of inspiration goes back to giving yourself time to listen to your inner voice and concentrate on what you are doing, so that you can see clearly and positively and know that your questions will be answered. If you are having a challenge with colors or pattern, just listen and take some time, and you will come up with the answer to that challenge. In other words, open your heart and listen, and the muse will speak to you!

Quilt Appraising

Have you ever watched something like *Antiques Roadshow* and wondered how those people can evaluate quilts and other old textiles? Quilt appraisal is both an art and science, but it can be learned.

Appraisers normally belong to an association (such as PAAQT, the Professional Association of Appraisers–Quilted Textiles). This group was founded in 1993 as a regulating body for quilt appraisers certified by the American Quilter's Society and offers classes and testing for those interested in a career as a quilt appraiser. You can find out more about them at quilt appraisers.org.

Quilt Appraiser Amy Korn

I interviewed AQS Certified Appraiser Amy Korn who decided in 2000 to become an appraiser in order "to encourage today's quilters to value their work more highly." Her passion for the work stems from "the anticipation of being presented with a quilt hidden in a pillow case and the excitement of wondering what will be revealed. I love the opportunity to share knowledge and expertise which may help quilt owners to value and preserve quilts for future generations."

Amy says, "Serving as an AQS certified appraiser of quilted textiles has deepened my appreciation of the art and craft of quilting. It has deepened ties with those women who spent hours at home working alone to create a masterpiece—or simply a bedcover to keep their families warm. Most quilts are ordinary, but each quilt has a story to tell."

Quilt History

A related occupation is that of quilt historian. These people seek to preserve the knowledge of quilts and quilting for future generations and study and help preserve antique quilts. Their knowledge of quilt patterns, various fabric patterns, and the history of quilting itself is a treasure to anyone interested in quilts and their preservation.

While many people think of old quilts as just faded, worn linens, many others study the fabrics, patterns, and techniques used in quilts of the past. This is a fascinating field that gives insight into the methods of fabric making and dying, and also offers a window into the lives of past quilters.

Quilt Historian Kimberly Wulfert

I spoke to quilt historian Kimberly Wulfert and asked her what led her to become a quilt historian. "It began with an interest in the women's motivation to work with small pieces of fabric in candlelight or sunlight to sew them into outstanding quilts," she said. "But soon after, my attraction to studying quilt history became all about the fabric and dating it, which meant learning about dyes and manufacturing of cloth and so on. This began my fascination with Indian, European, and American history primarily."

Kimberly says that viewing and examining old quilts makes her feel in touch with history itself, "especially with the women who were fighting for and supporting causes through cloth and needle. Women's opinions could be heard through quilts."

Kimberly points out that women often used their quilts to advocate for causes such as the temperance movement, political parties, and a variety of other social and political causes. In addition to naming quilt blocks after certain events or groups, many quilters would include poetry or prose about the topic of the quilt right on the blocks themselves. This allowed women to express themselves in a "soft" way that might not be noticed by men.

In order to become a quilt historian, a person would need to have "a driving interest in the reason behind something that occurs around quilting as an activity or is seen in quilts or textiles themselves. You do not have to be a quilt maker, or a history student. These may come in time, however, so watch out."

Kimberly says that when she personally makes quilts, she follows some basic rules to make sure that the textiles last a long time. "I keep them out of direct sunlight and lamplight. I include washing and care instructions when they are a gift. I don't think of quilts I make as having a future history as much as I attempt to emulate a prior history. I take steps to do that well, and then I take care of them to use for teaching purposes, not personal use, and include a label telling the motivation behind it and dates it reflects." Kimberly notes that she tries to make her reproduction quilts look like they really were produced in another era.

Kimberly adds, "Studying quilt history is rewarding in that a deep satisfaction is found in learning about the importance women played in America's growth and development as a young country. Women were extremely important in the events and outcome of political, military, educational, governmental, and of course family and the home practices through the last three centuries as it relates to their quilting activities."

Quilt Show Judging

Some quilters end up as quilt judges at shows. This is a difficult task because judges typically only get to look at a quilt for two to three minutes before passing judgment on it. Depending on directions from the show organizers, judges must focus on different aspects of the quilt, from design and artistry through technical details like stitching, mitering, and binding. Is this an art quilt show? Is the focus on machine quilting? Hand quilting? Appliqué?

Quilt show judges who want to be certified can go through an intensive program from the National Quilting Association (NQA). If they pass and are accepted as judges, they must "continue their education of current quilt-making techniques and judging procedures, follow the Judges' Code of Ethics, maintain their NQA membership, and submit an updated professional résumé and fee every three years to remain listed as an active certified judge."

Fame and Fortune

While I don't think you will ever become wealthy from quilting (and if you do, let me in on your secret), there are many people whose work is awarded by not only blue ribbons but sometimes prize money and the thrill of having quilts hung in galleries and museums, public buildings, and corporate offices.

My friend and fellow bee member Laurie Lynch has won several awards for her stunning hand-pieced, hand-quilted creations. She was kind enough to answer some of my questions.

When did you win your first award?

In 1998, about six years after I first started quilting, and it was the first show I ever entered. I won a second place in the bed-size/hand-pieced/hand-quilted category in our guild show.

What made you enter that particular quilt?

I liked the way it turned out. I'd combined several patterns to make something specific my dad had asked me for—a "blue quilt with bears on it." It was all handwork, and I thought it was good enough that I could handle having a judge comment on it. I also had the support and encouragement of my quilt bee, who are always more confident of my work than I am!

My other motivation was that I grew up in a rural hometown where the county fair was a major event every year. A lot of my classmates took entries in livestock or 4-H—baking, sewing, etc.—to the fair to be judged. I'd walk through all the barns and displays and be green with envy over my classmates who had these brightly colored satin ribbons hanging next to their name. I wanted one of those ribbons in the worst way! So now, many years later, I finally had my shot at that satin ribbon!

In fact, that quilt almost didn't appear in the show. I had already given it to my dad, and when I went home to bring it back for the show, it had slightly faded on the side that faced the window in their bedroom. I frantically called one of the show organizers and told her I had to withdraw the quilt; that it was not up to being judged. She talked me out of it. I think she actually told me the judges wouldn't care about the fading! Whether they did or didn't, you could have knocked me over when I saw that ribbon; I had already convinced myself I didn't have a chance.

Did winning an award make you feel differently about quilting in general?

Winning an award made me feel like I had finally found something I could excel at after years of dabbling in many different forms of needlework. And it was addictive! I could not wait to produce another show-worthy quilt and try my luck again. I wanted to work on my techniques and take some classes. At that point, I'd learned most of my quilting techniques from books, although my mother had taught me how to sew when I was in junior high school and I'd sewn my own clothes and theatrical costumes. The perk with quilts is that they don't have to fit my body, complement my skin tone, or hold up to thirty-second changes in murky light over a two-week performance schedule!

I was already enjoying the community of quilters—funny, creative, energetic, outspoken, supportive, strong women. I could travel to a new city by myself, attend a quilt show, and still find myself among friends. The award made me feel like I was fully participating in the quilt community.

When you make a quilt now, do you always have in the back of your mind whether or not it will be "good enough" for a show or do you just enjoy the process of making it?

Starting a new project, I'm just in it for the fun of it, playing with fabric, and patterns, and colors and choices. As the project progresses, I pay attention to how it's developing, whether I'm totally in love with the way it's going together, the way the pattern and colors work, whether my work on it is precise enough to stand up to scrutiny.

If I decide the project has the potential to submit for a show, I still enjoy the process, but I become more careful about the choices I make and the time I put into the work. I don't want to piece or quilt when I'm tired or distracted and end up with haphazard or sloppy work. I don't want to rush to a deadline and compromise the standard I've already established in the earlier stages of the quilt. But I also have to be careful not to let my decision to enter the resulting quilt in a show alter the choices I would make just because I think that choice would "judge better." In the end, I want that finished quilt to please me. I want to love it for my own reasons, not for what the judges may say or think about it.

Have the judges' comments led to changes in how you make your quilts? (Either esthetically or technically?)

They have, in positive ways. I've had helpful suggestions about areas that could be improved—binding technique, or piecing seam intersections, for example. I'm always curious going in to see what they will comment on, because I'm very aware of where the faults of my quilt are and I'm interested to see if they spot the same faults, or different ones! I've been very fortunate with judges who have made supportive comments and phrased their critiques in constructive terms as well.

Aesthetically, it's encouraged me to take more chances. One of my recent entries was a finalist in an award for best use of color, and the judges complimented my color choices. So I'm pushing the color envelope in my current project and trying combinations that previously I would not have been brave enough to even consider, let alone commit to fabric.

What would you say is the best part of entering a show (whether you win or not)?

I love seeing my quilt, many months of work finally completed, on display with all the other quilts and being a part of the creative energy of a show.

Unusual Quilting-Related Careers

In October of 2007 my quilt guild hosted Cathy Miller, also know as the Singing Quilter. I had heard of Cathy, but never heard her sing and I wondered what on earth there was to sing about when it came to quilting. Cathy is from Canada, as am I, and I loved hearing a voice from home. Her stories were funny, but her songs had me *crying* with laughter. I e-mailed Cathy the next day and on the way to her next gig in Houston she was kind enough to answer some questions for me.

How and when did you start your career as "the Singing Quilter"?

"In 1991 I was hired as a songwriter to write music for a play about quilting in Ottawa, Canada. It was a twenty-minute series of vignettes presented as part of Quilt Canada (our national quilt show). The playwright and I were non-quilters, but researched a lot. As part of my own research, I took a class in quilting, and became interested in it as a hobby."

In her presentation to my guild Cathy referred to that first quilt class as "the slippery slope"! Indeed that first class is the slippery slope for many people who just have a passing interest in quilting. If I had not taken a class and met other quilters, I probably would have dabbled in quilting for a while and then let it fall by the wayside like all my other crafty hobbies, but that one class opened up a whole new world to me. The right teacher and a good experience can mean the beginning of a lifelong love affair with quilting.

Cathy returned to her career and continued to dabble in quilting over the next several years.

"In 1999 my husband and I went to live in Darwin, Australia, for eight months (he was working as an engineer/town planner). To fill my time (I could not work, as I was there on a tourist visa), I took quilting classes and researched and wrote songs about quilting. We returned to Canada at the end of that time with enough songs for

a whole CD about quilting. It was released in September of 2000, and we've been on the road singing for quilting events ever since."

How has your approach to quilting changed because of your unique job?

Because I call myself the singing quilter, I almost *have* to make quilts to show during our performances. I think it has made me a more avid quilter—I certainly see thousands more quilts than I would have had I not been doing this. That means I have that many more inspirations for my own quilts. I don't feel the need to reproduce others' quilts, but I see lots of techniques which I try on my own quilts.

Aside from helping you to make a living, do you think that your songs encourage new quilters or help experienced quilters think of their art in new ways?

I consider myself a storyteller and a troubadour, bringing news about quilts and quilting from one area to another. I'm able to speak to beginner quilters and experts alike, and each has their own story to tell. I try to honor these stories by writing songs about them. I would hope to encourage everyone to keep meaning (and labels!) attached to their quilts, so their stories are kept intact.

I have had many people say they make their quilts while listening to my music. Some have made quilts based on my songs (such as *100 Ways to Hide Your Stash* and some of the history stories). One thing that may happen when people hear songs about quilting is that they take themselves more seriously—perhaps they think, "Well, she thinks this is important enough to write a song about, maybe it is!" It then becomes an affirmation to them.

Has quilting helped you to become more aware of your place in the universe? Have you ever used it to explore philosophical or emotional topics?

For me, quilting is another expression of my creativity. I have been a songwriter forever, it seems, and now I have another avenue through this visual art. It is all about emotion and learning. Each time one approaches a blank page or empty design wall, it's an adventure. There are creative decisions to be made at every turn, and the end product is not fixed until the label is on the quilt, or the song is recorded. What's lovely about having these two expressions is that if I've got writer's block, I can quilt, and vice versa. I have not yet made quilts to express philosophical or emotional topics directly, but perhaps the viewer can interpret these things for themselves.

Has quilting helped you get through any difficult times or events? Does it help you express happiness and joy?

I remember once, early in my quilting life, being terribly disappointed in not being included in a CD project that I had spent two years writing for. It's the most upset and angry I can remember ever being. I was in the middle of working on my first queen-sized quilt, and I remember being unable to do anything else but quilt. I got a lot done during that time, and it helped me to calm down and work through the emotions.

Quilting for me is a contemplative activity—unlike being on stage singing for people. It's when I'm deep inside myself: just me and the design and fabric, very much like when I write songs. It's when I'm on stage that I express the larger emotions like happiness and joy. That being said, I feel great joy when the design process is going well, and things are coming together beautifully. I don't express these things through my quilting, but I experience them while I'm quilting.

How do you see your music in relation to your quilting? How combined are they?

They are separate expressions of my creativity. I'm often asked if I sing while I'm quilting. I don't. Quilting is my hobby. Music is my profession that started as my hobby. They are both activities that I can continue to learn for the rest of my life. And they are both activities that can help me learn about myself for the same length of time. Neither of them can be entirely mastered, and that's why they hold my interest.

What is the best part of being the Singing Quilter?

Traveling to many parts of the world and meeting wonderful people who are creative, capable, and welcoming.

Do you have anything else to add?

I see so many similarities between creating fabric art and creating music. We have challenges and exercises to unblock our creative selves in music that are very similar to those in quilting. One of the most important pieces of advice for writing a song came from my mother (who was a sewer, not a musician). She said, "Never under-estimate the value of a cerise pillow in a white room." It means keep your art exciting, don't be afraid to surprise, be different and unique, step out on your own. My other important inspiration is *The Road Not Taken* by Robert Frost, which I discovered in eighth grade. "Two roads diverged in a wood and I, I took the road less traveled by, and that has made all the difference." By combining my passions for music and quilting, I feel I have forged a new direction for myself, and a more true and fulfilling life. I can't imagine anything better!

THREE

Quilts Around the World

Quilters affect eternity; they can never tell
where their influence stops.

—ANONYMOUS

Quilts are made on nearly every continent and in almost
every country. Countries such as Japan, the UK, New
Zealand, and Australia have strong and historic quilting traditions. Each culture views quilting in a unique way and this in
turn influences the quilters who grow up in that culture. And
quilting (both functional and artistic) has an ancient history.

One of the earliest examples of a quilted garment can be found
on the carved, ivory figure of a Pharaoh of the Egyptian First
Dynasty who is supposedly wearing a quilted mantle (c. 3400
BC). There are many references to quilts in literature, inventories
of estates and trade journals. In 1924, archeologists discovered a
quilted floor covering in Mongolia that is dated at somewhere
between the first century BC and second century AD

The earliest surviving bed quilt is from Sicily and dates back
to the 14th century. Made of linen and padded with wool, the
design features scenes from the legend of Tristan. It can be seen

at the Victoria and Albert Museum in London. (www.american quiltcompany.com/quilthistory.html)

So as you can see, quilting has been around for a while!

According to quilthistory.com/quilting.htm quoting Avril Colby, quilting "appears to have originated in Asia sometime before the first century CE. The first known quilted object is a quilted linen carpet dating from that time found in a Siberian cave tomb," with designs stitched into it. Even from the beginning, quilting served both practical and aesthetic purposes.

Colby continues, "Quilting does not appear to have been done in Europe much before the twelfth century, and is usually thought to have been brought back from the Middle East by the returning crusaders." However, a recent discovery from Germany indicates that quilted objects appeared in Europe far earlier: a Merovingian tomb from the fifth century contained a wool twill pall quilted with Egyptian cotton. The pall was an imported luxury item, but its presence shows that quilting was well established in the Mediterranean area.

By the fourteenth century, quilting armor was being made with quilted doublets and armor appearing in France, Germany, and England, and quilted tunics in Italy. Quilted jackets, often padded with metal plates, were used as a part of armor for soldiers in places like Paris and London. Domestic articles such as bed quilts may have been produced by professionals or household staff.

Again according to Colby, quilting may have even worked its way down to the lower classes by then; a tiny fourteenth-century Italian ivory shows St. Joseph, traditionally regarded as a peasant or lower-class artisan, wearing a diamond quilted tunic. Quilting had clearly become part of the European needlework tradition. (www.quilthistory.com/quilting.htm)

Even within one country, the variation in quilting styles is striking. In the United States there are several distinct quilting styles, including the simple beauty of Amish quilts, the elaborate Hawaiian appliqué quilts, the precise patterns machine pieced by the people of the Seminole nation, modern art quilts, and the rustic quilts such as those of the Gee's Bend quilters whose quilts were recently celebrated with their own line of stamps from the U.S. Postal Service (see pages 7–8).

This chapter will discuss how quilting differs depending on the country of origin and how quilters from different countries use different materials or techniques, or favor certain designs over others.

United States

Quilting did not exist in America until European settlers arrived. They brought quilts and the quilting tradition with them, and in some cases missionaries taught quilting to the native people they sought to "civilize." The oldest known quilt in the Unites States is the Saltonstall quilt, dated to 1704. This quilt utilized newspapers as a paper-piecing foundation and as the quilt wore out, the date on one of the newspapers was revealed.

Quilting spread out across America as the pioneers settled the country. Many quilt block designs date from the settling of America; they are identified by unique names that reflect the pioneer woman's daily life, such as Log Cabin, Churn Dash, and Hole in the Barn Door. Other block names reflect the hardship of the pioneer journey itself, such as Rocky Road to California.

Amish Quilts

Traditional Amish quilts are known for their use of solid-colored fabrics of black, brown, or other dark shades. This distinctive color combination comes in part from the Amish philosophy of living a "plain" life. They use muted colors and unpatterned fabrics, but their quilts are expertly quilted most often by hand, since traditional Amish shun most modern conveniences such as sewing machines. Some Amish quilts are machine pieced, but the quilting is done by hand and features elaborate and expert execution.

The Amish approach to quilting has evolved over the years. In their book *Decorative Arts of the Amish of Lancaster County*, Daniel and Kathryn McCauley write that "the Amish skepticism toward art did not result in rejecting beauty, but led instead to its refinement and simplification. The result has been the evolution of a decorative material culture that is neither over designed nor austere." While in the beginning Amish decorative art was not much different from that of their Pennsylvania German neighbors, the McCauleys say it was between 1850 and 1870 that the unique "Amish look" began to develop.

Amish people in different parts of the country also had different quilting traditions, with some areas producing quite different quilts than other areas. Amish quilt patterns include most of the traditional blocks, such as Log Cabin, but also very large scale motifs such as bars and a single diamond inside a square.

The Amish sell their quilts in shops, flea markets, auctions, and on the Internet, and some of them go for thousands of dollars. With recent interest in Amish quilts, even the designs themselves have changed, with the Amish people creating new designs and more elaborate quilting to appeal to the quilt-buying public. The popularity of these quilts was reflected in 2001 when the U.S. Postal Service released a series of stamps featuring traditional Amish quilt patterns.

Hawaiian Quilts

Quilting was introduced to Hawaiians in the 1820s by visiting missionaries. The Hawaiian people soon adapted the tedious cutting and piecing of traditional patchwork to a less wasteful method called appliqué.

The unique look of Hawaiian quilts is achieved by folding fabric squares into quarters or eighths and then cutting out a symmetrical shape, much in the way you would make a snowflake from a sheet of paper. These fabric shapes are then appliquéd onto a different-colored background fabric. Sometimes the appliqué is done in reverse, with the top layer cut away and the edges tucked under and sewn to create reverse appliqué that shows the bottom layer of fabric through a patterned "hole" in the top layer. (www.nvo.com/poakalani/historyofhawaiianquilting)

The shapes were often drawn directly onto the fabric, although most modern quilters use paper templates. Drawing directly on the fabric ensured that each pattern was completely unique and the patterns were closely guarded secrets. In fact, people who "borrowed" a pattern without authorization were chastened in public through songs!

Traditionally Hawaiian quilts use only two colors (often red and white), one for the background and one for the appliqué, although no one really knows why. It may have been due to a scarcity of different-colored fabrics.

Many believed that the spirit of the person creating and stitching the quilt became an integral part of the finished work, giving it an added dimension—a sense of life. It is suggested that because of this belief many of the earlier quilts made by the Hawaiian women had no openings in the central portion of the pattern of the design. This was so that the part of their spirit, which was considered a part of the quilt, could not wander. The belief caused many quilts to be burned upon the death of their creators, thus allowing their spirits to pass on with them in entirety. (Elizabeth Root—www.quiltshawaii.com/trad3.html)

Native American Quilting

The Seminole Indian tribe lived in the area that is now Georgia. In the early 1800s the tribe was forcibly resettled by Andrew Jackson on the orders of then-President James Monroe. After relocation, the Seminoles became traders and used bolts of cotton cloth to make clothing.

According to Victoria Westermark's *Many Bad Horses*, because travel was difficult and supplies hard to obtain, Seminole women made use of every scrap of material and began using thin, leftover strips of cloth to make decorative piecework. In the 1920s, the Seminoles obtained electric sewing machines and began selling their beautiful strip-pieced creations to tourists.

As their piecing skills increased, so did the intricacy of the designs, and Seminole women competed with each other to produce more beautiful work. The typical clothing of the Seminole people was elaborately decorated with these pieced designs.

Because women were the artists and because the Seminole nation (like many Native American groups) is matrilineal, the unique patterns created by each woman and handed down to her daughters eventually came to symbolize the different Seminole clans, or extended family groups. The history of the Seminole can be traced back by looking at the subtle changes in these clan patterns that occurred over the decades. Other designs depicted events or objects found in the artists' daily lives. Designs were sometimes named after the artist who created them, and copying a design was considered a compliment.

Over time, the Seminoles ceased wearing the patchwork clothes as everyday clothes, but still wear them for ceremonial and formal dress. The precision and beauty of these patterns makes them very popular with quilters even today.

Other native tribes also have very distinctive quilting styles. For example, several different plains tribes adapted the traditional Lone Star pattern to resemble the Morning Star pattern that they already produced in beadwork and paintings. This morning star (the planet Venus) was represented as an eight-pointed star made up of an intricate collection of tiny diamonds.

The Hopi, a southwestern tribe, also use traditional pottery and basket-weave patterns in their quilts. Traditionally a woven baby blanket was presented at the baby-naming ceremony. Nowadays the gift is just as likely to be a pieced quilt.

Books and quilt exhibitions have showcased Native American quilting in its many forms. And Native American women quilt for the same reasons many other women do—to create beautiful, heartfelt gifts for their family and friends and to celebrate special occasions. Gift giving is an important tradition in Native American tribes, and quilts make the perfect gift for nearly any occasion.

The Quilts of Gee's Bend

The town of Gee's Bend is on the site of former cotton plantations along the Alabama River near Selma, Alabama. The plantations, owned by Joseph Gee, were purchased by his relative Mark Pettway in 1850. Following the U.S. Civil War, the former slaves of the plantation became tenant farmers, worked for the Pettway family, and took the family name. This group was mostly isolated from surrounding areas and the quilts made by the women there are unique because of their situation as former slaves and the relative lack of interaction with other areas.

The quilts have been noted since the 1930s for their bold, distinctive style, and the women of the town have passed this approach to quilting down through six generations. The simple geometric designs have been compared to modern art; in 2002, the Houston Museum of Fine Arts exhibited seventy quilt masterpieces from the Bend, accompanied by two companion books, *The Quilts of Gee's Bend* and *Gee's Bend: The Women and Their Quilts.*

Japan

In Japan, a traditional quilting stitch is called *sashiko*. Starting in the eighteenth century, Japanese women made warm garments by sewing heavy fabric using fine running stitches; these stitches, meant to reinforce the clothing, later became decorative. When sashiko made its way into cities in the late nineteenth century, the stitching designs became elaborate and were used on other textiles besides clothing. (www.bettegant.com/sashiko.html)

Sashiko is a very spare, simple-looking way of quilting, but the simplicity of the designs gives it a beauty and dignity that is unique. It is generally done on whole-cloth quilts or clothing. Modern Japanese quilters often do very detailed, intricate piecework using minuscule pieces. *Taupes* (a catch-all word for a staggering variety of "muddy" or grayed-out fabrics) are very popular right now in Japanese quilting. These fabrics offer extremely subtle variations of tones and values, lending sophistication to the quilts.

Many Japanese quilters enter their work in international shows, and Japan has a large and growing community of quilters: the Tokyo International Great Quilt Festival in Japan attracted 245,000 visitors in 2002, the largest quilt festival attendance recorded to date!

Central and South America

Even in countries with warm climates like Panama, people quilt. *Molas* are intricate appliquéd patterns that are used to decorate the traditional blouses of women of the Kuna tribe. Most mola makers are women and, as in other matrilineal societies, this art and the special patterns created by each family are passed from mother to daughter. Some men are mola artists too.

Molas comprise two to seven layers of cloth sewn together; when part of each layer is cut away, a design emerges. The quilter then sews down the edges using tiny needles to produce the molas' distinctive fine stitching.

Traditional mola designs were taken from the geometric body art of the Kuna people. Modern mola patterns are derived from all sorts of influences, both modern and ancient. Mola collectors often use them as is, framing them as art. They can also be used in a variety of household items such as tablecloths, pillows, or placemats. They can also be used in the traditional way, to decorate clothing, and are often sold at quilt shows in the form of purses and handbags.

FOUR

Why Quilt?

We are all given talents, I do believe from the Great Creator.
To not use these talents would be an insult to God.

—ALEX ANDERSON

I grew up watching my mother and sisters sew garments. As I grew older, I helped, and when I was in junior high I learned the "proper" way to follow patterns. Even with the experience and instructions, my clothes sometimes came out looking awkward, and hemming pants to the proper length was completely beyond me. Don't even ask about the bathing suit I tried to make!

However, I always loved choosing the fabrics. Just going to the fabric shop, browsing the aisles and fondling all the different materials filled me with a unique mixture of eagerness and excitement. I loved the smooth, lustrous fabrics, the soft fuzzy fabrics, and the sheer, sparkly specialty fabrics. I could envision making something out of nearly every fabric I saw, but I never paid much attention to the plain cottons. Funny how all that changed when I discovered quilting! Once I started quilting, I gave up garment sewing almost completely, but I never stopped fondling fabrics.

I think this love of fabric is what made me fall in love with quilting. Now I have a reason to hoard dozens of yards of fabrics of every hue and texture, and I can fondle them any time I want.

I am often asked, "Why do you quilt? What's the big deal? What do you get out of it? What compels people to cut up perfectly good fabric and sew it back together?" This is my attempt to answer those questions and to explain why so many people are so mesmerized by the colors and patterns that they spend hours upon hours reading about, looking at, designing, piecing, and quilting quilts. What motivates and inspires them?

This chapter will explore the emotional, spiritual, and creative aspects of quilting. I will speak from personal experience and also feature a number of quilt artists, both well known and anonymous. These people will discuss what quilting is for them, how it helped them recover from illness, celebrate a milestone, heal from grief, share their creative vision, and help them explore their spirituality in new ways.

I drew on my friends and on several well-known quilters to find out what motivates them, inspires them, and drives them to keep on designing and making quilts even after they have been doing it for years and despite illness or physical limitation.

One of my favorite replies was from my friend Kim Harbin. When asked why she quilts, she laughs and says, "First question, and I was stumped. It's expressive? It's creative? It's cool? Then one day, while quilting, I realized I had a big smile on my face. I was alone! I quilt because it makes me happy!"

What better reason? In the end, everybody's reason for quilting boils down to what Kim says: it makes us happy.

When asked why *she* quilts, Alex Anderson replies, "This is an interesting question. I have never been asked, because I see quilting as a lifestyle. When you get it, you get it; when you don't, you don't. It has always been fun watching the producers, camera people, etc., roll their eyes when they hear they are working on a quilting show; and then by the end of the production they're excited to come back next season. It is an experience!"

As Alex pointed out, the love of quilting definitely spreads virally. The slightest amount of interest in my quilting leads me to want to "convert" the non-quilter by teaching her how to quilt and encouraging her to go to quilt shows and shop hops. Sometimes it works, and sometimes it doesn't. When it does, I've made a new quilting buddy. When it doesn't, I have at least spread the knowledge of quilting a little bit farther.

Creative people often try several different arts and crafts

Shops Hops are usually annual events arranged by a group of quilt shops within several miles of one another to increase sales and attract new customers. The last shop hop I went on led me on a three-hundred-mile journey around west Michigan. Each shop has special sale items just for the participants. Normally each shop gives away a pattern or kit and a block pattern. The shops also design a quilt specifically for that year's hop, which may have a special theme. When you collect and assemble all the blocks, you have that year's shop-hop quilt. Sometimes you get a special discount for completing the hop and visiting all the shops. Shop hops are a great way to spend a weekend with your quilt buddies doing what you love best—fondling fabric, shopping, and socializing.

There are virtual Internet-based shop hops too: instead of driving for hours and hours, you merely click from one shop to the next. Typically the shops hide a little icon (usually a bunny) somewhere on their website. You have to search around a bit to find it, then you enter your e-mail address for a chance at the grand prize. They usually give away sewing machines as top prizes and have several smaller prizes too. Unlike real-life shop hops, online hops can feature hundreds of shops (and save you wear and tear on your car!).

before they find one that feels right to them, one that holds their interest beyond the latest fad. In my lifetime I've tried drawing with oil pastels, sewing garments and household accessories, cross-stitching, tole painting, rug hooking, and beadwork. But when I found quilting, all those other interests fell by the wayside. It consumed me utterly in a way that none of these other activities ever did. And that interest has been sustained for more than ten years already. This same kind of progression through a variety of creative and artistic pastimes holds true for many of the quilters with whom I spoke.

Kim Harbin says, "I have a BFA and MA in elementary education. My major concentration was in clay. I was exposed to a wide variety of media. I am confident in art—loved experimenting with various media. Had to make money to live—I knew I could not survive on my own/[my]own art. [I] love teaching."

She continues, "But something was always missing—not quite right—right place, wrong time . . . wrong place, right time. Through a long line of events I discovered quilting. I am home! I am where I am supposed/should be. Quilting makes me happy! Sew many quilts (possibilities) . . . 'Sew' little time."

Caryl Bryer Fallert says, "I've been an artist my whole life. I tried many different mediums, and when I discovered that I could make art with cloth, I found my heart. It is the most expressive medium for the images I want to create."

Alex Anderson tells her story. "In college, I thought I was going to be a weaver for life (it was an acceptable form of art); however, when I saw a quilt show in Oakland, I realized that quilting could be viewed as art, and at that moment I was hooked for life."

M'Liss Rae Hawley quilts in order to share the joy of quilting with others. Each time she designs a new quilt, she ensures that it is simple enough for quilters of all skill levels to make. When she gives a quilt away to a family member or friend, she enjoys the fact that the quilt has a well-documented history (through being featured in one of her books). Most quilts have little if any historical or reference material attached to them, and part of M'Liss's joy is knowing that the recipients of her quilts (and future historians) have all the data available to them.

My friend Joyce DenBleyker has a very practical reason for quilting. "Since my job is very analytical, quilting provides me with a creative balance." Joyce and I both work in information technology, and I share her sentiment. When you just can't look at one more spreadsheet, when you think that next e-mail will push you over the edge, shutting the door on your quilt studio (if you're lucky enough to have one), or sitting at your work table and looking at your fabric and projects can clear your mind like nothing else.

Beth Ann Williams says she quilts "because I can't *not* do it! It is part of me. It is joy and pain and freedom and love."

Making Connections

Quilting brings people together, sometimes from all over the world, and sometimes only virtually. Local bees and guilds are obvious gathering places for quilters, but there are also Internet chat rooms, newsgroups, mailing lists, classes, and virtual bees and guilds made up of people who never meet face-to-face. These virtual quilt groups hold round-robins, fabric swaps, block exchanges, and even virtual shop hops where you visit online quilt shops to collect points or prizes while shopping.

Quilt University (quiltuniversity.com) offers classes from nearly forty teachers from around the world. It runs several classes from January until the end of October. The classes include written lessons, forum discussions, and a student photo gallery.

This is a great way to take classes if you are homebound or don't live near a quilt shop!

Online Quilt (onlinequilt.net) is a collaborative art community whose members create and share digital images. These quilts are not made of fabric at all, but are collaborative collages where each artist creates a tiny portion of the whole (think of a tile in a mosaic). You reserve a tile, download it to your computer, and use a paint program (such as Photoshop) to draw whatever you want on your tile. The quilts have themes and when you get your tile you can see a small portion of the surrounding art, so you can make your piece blend in with those around it.

Fab Shop Hop (fabshophop.com) has been hosting online shop hops for several years now. Quilters are given a list of online quilt shops to visit. Once at a shop, you must search for the Fab Shop Hop bunny icon. Click the icon to register that shop and prove you've been there. If you collect the required number of bunny icons, you are eligible for prizes such as new sewing machines. Just like in a real shop hop, of course, the fun of shop hopping is shopping along the way, and the prizes are usually secondary in importance.

The Quilt Show (thequiltshow.com) is a newer website started by Alex Anderson and Ricky Tims. This site includes a chat forum, blogs, and *The Quilt Show*. The site also has contests and prizes, a shop, and a quilt gallery. It is one-stop-shopping for quilters where you can chat with like-minded people and enjoy your hobby from the comfort of your home.

If you prefer interacting with real-life quilters (and we *are* a fun bunch), you can find a great list of guilds around the world at Quilt Guilds (quiltguilds.com). This is where I found a local guild after I moved to southwest Michigan.

One of my favorite ways to connect with other quilters is at a twice-yearly quilting retreat founded by members of my quilting

bee. It started small with just sixteen women and by the following spring we had more than thirty attending. We had our fif-
teenth quilt camp in March 2008. I met my friend Kim, an
elementary-school art teacher, at that retreat. Kim says, "To be
with others that speak my language, that do what I do . . .
months of therapy just in a mere three days. The laughs and fel-
lowship—priceless!"

This may be one of the hardest things to explain to people
about our retreat. It doesn't really matter how much quilting we
get done. Just to be around other creative and artistic women, to
be free of deadlines and childcare and the demands of husbands,
homes, jobs, and the outside world, is a blessing. We can be
among people who won't tell us that quilting past three o'clock
in the morning must be a sign of sickness. We can relax, be our-
selves, and do what we love among others who are doing the
same. I have to agree with Kim—it's better than therapy.

In fact, the best part of quilting for me has been the friendships
that have developed as a result of it. In addition to the quilting
(and other crafts) we get done at our bees or retreats, we get to
know each other in a way that is rare in modern life. In the hus-
tle and bustle of work, childcare, social engagements, and
appointments, it is rare to just sit for hours and talk to a friend.

At the most recent quilt retreat I observed as much laughter as
ever, and also a huge amount of caring and support for those
going through pain (both emotional and physical), and celebration for some of us who have cause to celebrate. The girls threw
me a surprise bridal shower and I was completely floored. I'm a
bit on the shy side and although I have a couple of close friends
in that group I had no idea so many of them would take part in a
party for me. I was really touched.

Without quilting to bring us all together, many of us would
have far fewer friends and a much lonelier existence. Many in

our group are single for one reason or another, and our friendships with other women are what carry us through the rough times. Our shared love of quilting gives us the opportunity to get to know each other and form bonds that have lasted for years.

Traditions and Legacy

The modern world is full of stress, and it seems to get worse with each passing year. No matter how peaceful your own individual life may be, the tension of the outside world has its way of leeching in. Even the products we buy are not of the quality they once were. Mass-produced factory clones fill our homes, and few people can afford handmade quality anymore. Quilting provides a way for some of us to hark back to an earlier era, an age when taking time to make something well was appreciated. And in doing so, we hope that our creations will be cherished and passed down. For some quilters, this is part of why we quilt: to leave a legacy and share a tradition with future generations. In addition, just performing the same actions as our foremothers, going through the same motions, sometimes brings us peace and fulfillment.

Susan Towner-Larsen says in *Within Sacred Circles*, "Sometimes when all else in life feels out of control or overwhelming, the connection to fabric and design, the familiar rocking motion of stitching, and the spiritual, intimate realization that my foremothers shared the same comfort, re-ground and center my soul. When each stitch is a prayer, or even when each stitch is a release of stress or anger, the sense of sacredness of life begins again to seep into my consciousness . . . Quilting often has the mysterious sense of 'coming home,' which I have come to recognize as the return to God, to myself, and to the matters of the world from a position of wholeness or centeredness."

It is this feeling of wholeness that keeps people coming back to quilting, even in a world as harried and scattered as ours.

A member of my local quilt guild Cindy Shepherd says, "I quilt to give my descendants something to pass on to their children, just as my grandma did."

She relates this story from her childhood: "When I was a little girl, I lived on a farm. We had a flock of sheep that were sheared each spring. My grandmother would take the wool from our prize ram and send it in to be cleaned and processed into a quilt batting. Each year one family member would receive a handmade quilt from Grandma. My mother sewed clothing and would save all the cotton scraps for Grandma's quilts. We would look for fabric in the quilts of blouses and dresses to identify whose they were. Being Grandma's godchild, I received the first of these quilts, and my youngest son received her last."

Some other quilters have not planned that far in advance. When asked if she plans to leave quilts as a legacy for her children, Alex Anderson replies, "Let's just get them married first!"

Caryl Bryer Fallert feels that her quilts, which hang in several museums, will be her legacy, since she has no children.

I am also childfree and, while none of my quilts are likely to ever hang in a museum, I do carefully label each one just in case some quilt historian comes along and wants to investigate my growing pile of work. Caryl told me that she sells most of her quilts, seeing them like adult children—born, raised, and now sent off on their own into the world. (This also gives her more space in her studio—I think she's onto something there.)

When M'Liss Rae Hawley is asked about leaving a legacy, she says, "I look at everything I do as being passed down to my children and my children's children." She doesn't sell her quilts, but makes them as gifts; so she looks at everything she does as heirloom. Having her quilts published gives the recipient the story and history behind a quilt, whereas many quilts don't have a history.

Healing

Some quilters turn to quilting to help them heal from an injury or illness. Some use the expressiveness of the quilting medium to communicate their helplessness, pain, suffering, or healing through quilting. Sometimes quilting is all you have to hang onto in a world that has suddenly been turned upside down by illness.

Sue Reno says, "I made a quilt, Skunk Cabbage and Possum, while undergoing a rocky recovery from surgery. I was often in pain and frustrated by the length of the healing process, and working on the quilt was difficult, but I persevered because making the quilt was a process I could control, and I was driven to bring some normality into my daily life. And even though this quilt has skull imagery in it, it turned out to be a very cheerful and life-affirming work."

Other quilters expressed similar sentiments. Sometimes these healing quilts lead to unexpected surprises. In 1983, Caryl Bryer Fallert was in an accident and had a brace on her leg. It was January in Chicago. She faced six weeks of being housebound in the winter during her recuperation. She had just been to a lecture where she discovered the phenomena of art quilts. Confined to a rolling office chair, she made Red Poppies, her first art quilt and first completely original design. She sent if off to the first quilt show she ever entered and it got an award! That quilt is now in MAQS, the Museum of the American Quilter's Society.

Angie Crosson says that her love of quilting helped her "want to do what the doc said so I could get out of bed faster and get back to quilting."

Quilting can sometimes help people overcome emotional troubles. Linda Hall relates, "I suffered a heart attack and the doctor told me I can expect some mild depression afterwards. I had wanted to study fiber art and mixed-media quilting more deeply for two years, and I found an online venue that could teach me what I wanted to learn. I used my recovery time to build up binders full of studies and samples—doing 'gymnastics' with mixed media to eventually use in my art quilts. I did not suffer any depression at all, and decided that if I have another heart attack, I will die quilting."

Mary Ann Titus writes that the process of quilting helped her heal "the same way that writing poetry helps. To be able to articulate the pain, to call up the healing, to remember who one is outside the illness or the injury, to mine the deep compassion that connects us in our pain with all who are in pain. It enlarges us."

Some artists use their art to raise awareness of diseases that affect them. Sandy Shelenberger writes, "I have also designed two 'art bras' that toured the country as part of a Way to Women's Wellness, with the proceeds going to breast cancer research and treatment. I had biopsies that were benign, but it made me aware of how prevalent breast cancer is and I wanted to do something to support that cause. One of my art bras was in the 2007 Way to Women's Wellness Art Bra Calendar and it makes me feel good that my artwork has brought awareness and hope to many women."

Celebrations

Many people create quilts to celebrate milestones or good fortune. Duet #2 was made by Caryl Bryer Fallert after her husband's first stroke in 1995. They said he was unlikely to be able to speak or walk or get out of bed, but he proved them wrong and was out of the hospital in five days, walking with a cane; he was later able to hunt, fish, go to Alaska, and travel all over the world for eleven years after the first stroke. The quilt features two soaring eagles swirling over one of Caryl's trademark hand-dyed multi-colored backgrounds, and it won the Pfaff Master Award for Machine Artistry at the International Quilt Association show in Houston in 1997.

> Quilts should make you smile and [be] happy and think that you can do that. There is so much sadness in the world—I want to be in the zone and not dwelling on the unhappy events . . .
>
> —M'LISS RAE HAWLEY

Alex Anderson celebrated her fiftieth birthday by making a quilt. "I was totally surprised when presented with a set of blocks from quilting friends across the country. Originally it was to have been given as a quilt, and thankfully it was just the blocks. The joy of piecing that quilt was indescribable. The piecing process was joyful, creatively challenging, and a blast from beginning to end."

Creativity

> The soul should always stand ajar,
> ready to welcome the ecstatic experience.
>
> —EMILY DICKINSON

Sue Reno says, "Everything I do is totally unexpected. If I didn't have the capacity to surprise and delight myself, there would be no point to this activity. While I may start with some imagery I am interested in, and pick potential colors and fabrics, the design and construction of my quilts is done improvisationally. If I had to have a plan, and then stick to it, I would be bored to tears. There's plenty of routine and humdrum activity in everyday life; quilting is my escape from it. If this wasn't fun, I wouldn't be doing it!"

Sue says that she taps her creative potential "through introspection and observation: the first step is to listen closely to your inner voice and figure out what is important to you and why you want to express it in fabric. The next step is to figure out the techniques and processes that will allow you to do so. My slogan is that technique should be the servant of intent. I think that playing around with various techniques is like practicing scales on the piano; useful in its way, but not the true expression of the potential of the medium."

Sue is not the only quilter who likes to strike out on her own when it comes to design. One of my favorite quilts is one called Left to My Own Devices, which I designed for a round-robin in my quilt bee.

I have always wanted to create a Mariner's Compass quilt, but the pattern, with its intricate points and precise piecing, was beyond my technical capabilities. But I had my heart set on making the mariner's compass the center of my round-robin quilt, so I looked at every pattern I had for this block and studied books that discussed it.

I've done a lot of machine appliqué, and I finally had the thought that cutting out the pieces and appliquéing them down would *have* to be easier than piecing them. Piecing would require lining up the sharp points of the bias-cut triangles. Appliqué would allow me to just fuse the pieces to the background, eliminating the need for piecing.

Using my favorite fabrics from the Fossil Ferns line by Benartex, I pieced the triangles out of light and dark values of yellow,

A round-robin is an event that can take months to complete. The rules vary, but for this particular round-robin, each person had to make a center block of about twenty by twenty inches. It could be any pattern, color, or style we wanted. One person kept track of the order in which we had to pass our quilts around, and we each had to add one border to each quilt. We exchanged quilts monthly and when the time came to show the new border, the owner of the quilt being shown had to leave the room. The grand unveiling was at our annual Christmas party.

The anticipation was awful! We had a whole year of wondering what our bee sisters were doing to "our" quilts! At each monthly "showing," we'd wait in turn outside the room listening to the oohs and aahs and sometimes laughter as our quilts were unveiled. We took a photo of each woman with the quilt so we had a record of who had added which border.

It was fun to see the different styles. Some of the centers were traditional blocks. Some were flowery and lacey. They all reflected the women who had made them and it was easy for us to see each other in our quilts. My own was fairly wild in both color and design, at least by the standards of my bee.

purple, teal, and magenta. I made the points asymmetrical and bordered them with black bias binding to hide the raw edges. That worked fine, except that the bases of the points didn't form a perfect circle as they should have, and the ends of the bias tape stuck out awkwardly into the center. I wanted to use a brilliant yellow in the center, but the bias showed right through it. I was stuck and thought I'd have to start all over again or choose a different block to make. It was so frustrating! I didn't want to waste my beautiful fabric (not to mention the time I had already invested in the quilt), so I sat and thought and flipped through countless books and magazines looking for some technique that would rescue it from the UFO pile.

It finally struck me that I could use black in the center. The colorful compass points reminded me of a black hole exploding outward, if there is such a thing. I appliquéd it onto a pale blue background and sent it off to the bee to see what they would do to it. The first woman added a triple border of two narrow black stripes with a multicolored stripe of Fossil Ferns between them. The next border used traditional flying geese blocks and a multi-hued striped fabric. The next woman added another narrow black border and a purple and teal fabric with images that resembled fireworks exploding. The next border was very wide and black and featured asymmetrical stripes of multicolored bias tape. The outer border was just one strip of fabric, but it featured a modern-looking pattern of repeated multicolored circles. When the quilt was finally revealed to me at the end of the round-robin, I was thrilled with it!

While designing the central block for the project I was listening to my favorite Pet Shop Boys CD, and the song "Left to My Own Devices" seemed the perfect name for this quilt that was like nothing I had ever seen before.

Quilting in the Zone

Athletes often talk of being "in the zone." Usually this means being in such a state of concentration on the here and now—on the task at hand—that you don't even notice the passage of time. What was difficult becomes easy, what was work becomes play, and you never want to stop.

You don't have to be an athlete to feel it, though. It's easy to while away the hours if you are doing something you love—chatting with a friend, reading a book, quilting . . . Whether designing, piecing, or stitching, quilting can provide that same sense of being at one with the universe. I have spent many seemingly short days in my studio, especially when I am designing a new quilt or choosing the fabrics. I go downstairs in the morning, then look up and it is supper time already!

I am not the only one to have this experience. "When in the flow, I feel excitement and exceeding joy," says Roslyn Besterman. "The piece is no longer mine. It becomes a co-creation. Even with traditional quilts there is a connection to all the other women who have made the same patterns but with other fabrics."

Others express similar feelings. "It is a feeling of sheer joy or excitement. It is euphoria!" exclaims Marlene Brown Woodfield.

JoAnn Perkins notes, "It's always a good feeling when you are 'in the zone' and everything just falls into place. I find I just lose all track of time and can work into the late hours, particularly if I am home alone. I do enjoy putting on music and maybe that helps to get me into that state of mind."

"I *love* that zone—it is a state of complete surrender, reflection, and joy," adds Alex Anderson. And Kim Harbin says, "Wow! Wow! Wow! It's like for just a small time that nothing else matters. I don't do anything in particular to get there. A glass of wine and good music helps. I just know that when I get to the zone, interruptions make me nuts!"

Adrienne Alexander agrees. "I must admit: I zone out when I am quilting more than I zone in. Quilting can put me in a special place where there are few worries or cares. I don't do anything in particular to go there, it just happens."

Other artists say that they don't think they ever get to this point. Some cite a lack of technical skill, while others just did not seem to make it into that state. I believe that once your technical skills reach a certain level (whatever you consider to be "good enough"), then it is easier to slip into the zone.

M'Liss Rae Hawley expresses a similar sentiment. She says that it goes back to giving yourself time to listen and concentrate on what you are doing so that you can see clearly and positively that your questions will be answered. If you are having a challenge with colors or pattern, just listen and take some time, and you will come up with the answer to that challenge. She says that she tells quilters to "try more, do more, and be more creative, because you're going to get better, and the more confident you are in your skills, the easier you can get into the zone the more you will enjoy it."

She isn't finished. "It doesn't matter what your wife or children or husband or anybody says—you are pleasing yourself. This industry is a forum for women whose voices will never be heard. There aren't many industries where women can stand up and say, 'Look what I did.'" M'Liss says that her forum is the world because she's putting her quilts in books. She adds, "If you can realize that you can make people happy with your work, it is a life-changing experience."

One final note on creativity . . . My friend Adrienne points out that many quilt patterns go to great pains to tell you how to assemble the quilt, but then you see those dreaded words, *quilt as desired.* As she sees it, if she could quilt it "as desired," it would look like something by Irma Gail Hatcher! (Irma Gail is an author and quilt teacher. You can see some of her creations on her website at irmagailhatcher.com.) Adrienne says, "Eventually we learn that quilting is our unique way of expressing our creativity and that's what makes it special. I may never be able to quilt like Irma Gail Hatcher, but there is nothing to keep me from trying!"

Spirituality

People see spirituality in many different ways. For some it means following an organized religion. For others it means seeking your own path and picking and choosing the elements from various religions that work for you. For some it means celebrating the wonders of the natural world and using the inherent energy of the universe to feed your creative passion.

Spirituality is often represented in quilts, especially those given as gifts for weddings, baptisms, and other events.

I asked a few quilters about this topic and their answers were varied and interesting. Some people pray while quilting, some meditate. I personally love to sing while designing; some people think positive thoughts and try to imbue the stitches with love and good energy. Alex Anderson says that she does "all of the above—sometimes even dance!" (Me too, Alex!)

Beth Ann Williams says, "Art making in general and quilt making specifically are important aspects of my own spiritual practice. This is not to mean that I don't ever just go up to my studio and mess around for fun! But expressing my creativity provides a way for me to mirror the creative activity of the divine. It can also be a form of prayer that is more accessible to me than verbal expression. Sometimes my heart is too full to be able to express myself coherently in a formal, verbal manner. But my struggles and joys always show up in my artwork—whether I recognize the messages right away, or unravel them long after the work has been completed."

Caryl Bryer Fallert says that she studied Ram Dass meditation/yoga, which advocates letting your work be your meditation. "When I machine quilt, it is all stream of consciousness and improvisation, focused on making it as beautiful as possible. I feel like this is when I'm connecting to the spiritual. I get totally involved in making the stitches flow, and in making every swirl and pattern as beautiful as possible. My quilting is almost all stream of consciousness. I just put the quilt under the needle and make up the pattern as I go."

Quilter's Spaces

A quilter's work space is an important aspect of the work. It can be hard to totally immerse yourself in a creative pursuit if you are surrounded by chaos and noise.

Some quilters have achieved amazing results with little to no space. Author and quilter Paula Nadelstern is widely known for creating her amazing kaleidoscope quilts in her tiny New York City apartment in the Bronx. On her website, Paula says, "For over twenty years, my work space in our two-bedroom apartment was the forty-inch-round kitchen table. A long-distance view, alternate space, or not making quilts were not options." Like generations of quilters before her, Paula made do with what she had, and her love of the art and her unique style led to a whole career as a quilt designer, author, and teacher.

Beth Ann Williams says, "I treat my studio as sacred space. It is private; no one is allowed in without an invitation. I surround myself with images, colors, textures, etc., that inspire and nurture me. Everything I need is close at hand. Carefully selected music helps set the tone—whether it's joyfully boisterous, edgy, mournful, or soothing. And I always have a good supply of chocolate on hand."

Until Beth said this, I had never considered keeping my studio private. When I started quilting, I sat on the floor and used the coffee table for cutting and sewing. I was surrounded by people: my then-husband, my cats, and whatever friends dropped by. When I moved to a small two-bedroom house, I used a desk in a corner of the living room and kept my stash in a closet in another room (with a few choice fabrics tucked into the CD rack in the living room because they were pretty). While sitting at my desk I had to tolerate whatever my boyfriend was watching on TV. When I moved to a three-bedroom ranch, I could finally devote an entire room to my sewing, but it still was not a sacred space and was not completely private.

Now I am in a larger home and have one room that has all the space I need for designing, pressing, cutting, sewing, and rearranging blocks; I still let my cats keep me company, and sometimes my boyfriend will come upstairs and play with them just to give me peace and quiet. But when I am starting a project, it's just me and the fabric. I need to be alone to select colors. I need solitude as I arrange and rearrange the blocks on my design wall. And I crave that alone time.

M'Liss Rae Hawley has a similar take on her studio. It is private inasmuch as it's in her home and strangers don't come traipsing through; but her husband and assistant come in, as do occasional friends. But when she wants to create, M'Liss turns off the TV, stereo, and phone, and avoids all external distractions. She doesn't even have a clock in there. M'Liss feels that being alone with your thoughts in this way is what puts you in that place of feeling positive, thankful, and creative—in the zone.

If you have a lot of external things going on, you can't focus on the color, thread, patterns, fabric, cutting, stitching, quilting, embellishment, and embroidery. To M'Liss, the sound of her sewing machine is like "vacation." Her studio is a sanctuary, a place to come home to after traveling. It is the place where she can get into the zone or that private place.

Some quilters have traveling studios. Many quilters are snowbirds and travel south for the winter. These quilters outfit their motor homes as studios, fitting their machines and as much of their stash as they can into their temporary living space.

FIVE

My Own Story

The best part of quilting are the friendships you make.

—KELLY SMITH

I've been writing about other people's experiences and realize now that I've not included my own thoughts. At first I thought I should be more detached—but I'm a quilter, too! So with that in mind, I decided to answer my own questions. My reasons may not be as philosophical as some, but then again, a lot of the quilters I interviewed thought they had nothing to say! Once I'd read their stories, I told them otherwise. Nearly every letter I received had some gem of wisdom in it. Maybe mine will too.

Kelly Smith Speaks

Why do you quilt?

I quilt mainly for the companionship of other quilters. When I first moved to the United States I didn't know anyone aside from my boyfriend. The people at work were all busy with their own friends and families, and I had no one with whom I could share a common interest. Joining a quilting bee gave me a ready-made group of women with similar artistic interests. We were from different backgrounds, and I don't think they knew what to make of me at first. For one thing, I was about ten years younger than the youngest of them; they mostly had children, and most of them were married. I think they thought I was exotic! They were shocked that I had met my boyfriend on the Internet, for example, and worried that he might turn out to be an ax murderer. They were amazed that I had just picked up and moved to another country, to a state I'd never even visited before, to start a job in an industry I'd never worked in. Eventually we got to be good friends, and if I ever leave Michigan I'll be sad to leave them behind. So, the companionship of other quilters is a big reason why I continue to quilt.

When I start a brand-new quilt, I get completely sucked into the thrill of designing it (or tweaking the design if I'm using a commercial pattern), and I can spend hours and hours just auditioning new fabrics and moving blocks around until the arrangement looks good to me.

This time spent alone in my quilt room is an important element in maintaining my sanity. I am generally a loner and cherish my solitude. When I was single I spent a lot of time alone, even when I had roommates, and I find that I am more creative when I have time to sit and reflect. Sometimes just looking at the fabrics and colors suggests a pattern, or helps me work through a particularly vexing bit of construction.

What keeps you interested in quilting after all these years?

I've always loved color. I love to color pictures, make puzzles, draw on the computer, and just about anything else that lets me use color. A couple of weeks ago I bought a book called *Watercolor 101* and when I'm done writing this book I'm going to start teaching myself the basics of watercolor painting.

I am also a very tactile person. I can't walk through a fabric shop without fondling all the different fabrics. I've heard a lot of quilters say that part of the reason they became quilters is because they had to do *something* to justify all the fabric they were buying! I fall into that category. I can't resist the patterns, textures, and hues, and I must bring them home to love them up close. There are some fabrics that are so gorgeous I know I will never cut them up. Instead, I might just stretch them on a frame and hang them as art.

Also, being in the bee keeps me interested. I get to learn from the more advanced quilters in the group—we have a couple of award winners in our midst—and I sometimes get to teach things I know that no one else has tried, like handdying and sun-painting fabric.

> Sun painting is a technique of using photo-reactive dyes to imprint the outline of objects like leaves, flowers, and other interesting shapes onto fabric. You can find all the supplies you need to do this, from fabric to dyes, at dharmatrading.com.

The best thing about a bee is that we each have unique interests and talents. For example, my color choices are probably the most "out there" of the group, and even though not all the others would choose those colors, they are very supportive of the projects I make. Others in the group are avid hand piecers and quilters, and even though I have no desire to learn hand piecing or hand quilting, I really love the gorgeous quilts they make. Some of the ladies in the group use more subdued colors and make more traditional quilts, and seeing their work has made me appreciate those just as much as any vivid art quilt. Belonging to a bee opens your eyes to aspects of quilting that you may never have considered before.

Have the skills and temperament needed to be a quilter made other parts of your life easier to cope with? (Stress, grief, joy, etc.)

Hmm. This question is easier to ask than to answer. I don't know that there is a specific "quilter's" temperament. Some of us are very impatient to see the finished top, and then lose interest. Others love all aspects of quilting. Some of us don't worry too much over a cut-off point or a slightly crooked seam. Others will take their work apart ten times until it is perfect.

One thing that a lot of us have in common is a love of showing others how we did what we did. Show-and-tell is a big part of just about any gathering of quilters as we all share our latest treasures and creations. Explaining my quilting methods to others certainly helped me become more at ease in teaching in general. I've taught adults and children how to do simple quilting tasks like cutting, piecing, choosing fabric, machine appliqué, and so on. The more I do it, the more I enjoy it.

Some quilters are very shy about showing their work, even when it is absolutely gorgeous. I show mine even when I know it's less than perfect, because if I didn't, I'd never show anything. One of my interviewees—M'Liss Rae Hawley—thinks that if you don't show your work to others, you are missing out on a life-changing experience.

Do you feel that quilting helps you be more in tune with nature or God? How so?

As an atheist, I'd have to say no to this question. But having said that, I do believe there is a spirit or consciousness that infuses the natural world. From my point of view, it is impossible to stand in the Rocky Mountains or beside the ocean and not feel the vibrations of the universe. Since I have not made many art quilts, I can't say that my work has really been influenced by this feeling, but I can fully understand others who tap into it in their work.

Is quilting a meditative activity for you?

Not in the strictest sense. I don't have the patience for meditation, and I've tried!

How does it feel when you are quilting and you know you are "in the zone" or flow? Can you describe that feeling? Do you do anything in particular to get to that state?

Now this, I recognize. I have spent many hours happily designing, drawing, coloring, auditioning fabric for, cutting, and piecing quilts. The actual quilting part is work for me, not play, and as a result I have *dozens* of unfinished tops!

I am not sure how to describe this feeling. It is a state of being totally present in the moment, completely focused on what I am doing to the point that I don't notice the passage of time. I don't notice that I am getting stiff, sore, tired, and hungry. I don't notice that I should be putting supper on, or that the sun is going down. I am just completely focused on the work at hand. When I do realize I have to stop, I'm always cranky and pouty!

I love the "in the zone" feeling when it arrives (it does not always) and would love to have the luxury of time to quilt more often so that I could experience this more often. The only other times I've felt this way are when I've been reading a very absorbing book, walking in the woods, or doing something sensual and tactile like giving or receiving a massage.

One reason I go on my twice-annual quilting retreats is so that I can sew without worrying about the time. Aside from set mealtimes and a couple of planned activities like show-and-tell, we are free to work all night and all day if we want. Some of the ladies stay up until three or four in the morning on a regular basis. I'm not much of a night owl, but even I have been up sewing until one or two a.m. on a few occasions.

If you teach, does teaching quilt classes and retreats give you a similar feeling? Is that as satisfying as quilting, or is it a totally different experience?

I have taught some people to quilt and also to do other quilt-related things, like hand-dying and sun-painting fabric. The satisfaction I get from teaching is completely different from what I get out of quilting on my own. For one thing, quilting is generally a solitary activity. Even if I'm in a room at the retreat with thirty other women, I am working on my own thing and not interacting with them except during breaks.

Teaching is, by necessity, a social, communal activity. I learn as much from the students as I do from teachers when I take a class. Seeing them make the same mistakes I made, or hearing them ask the same questions, reminds me of how far I've come—and compared to some, I haven't come far at all. I enjoy sharing my knowledge, and I love the expressions of joy when others create something unique and personal.

If someone just could not understand your motivation for quilting, what would you tell them to explain why it is important to you?

I would tell them that it feeds my creative monster. Before I found quilting, I tried a variety of crafts, sewed my own clothes (badly), wrote poetry (even worse), and wrote fiction. Now that I'm a quilter,

I have one hobby that can include all my passions—I get to play with fabric and make something beautiful and useful, unlike the ugly, ill-fitting clothes I used to make. I get to draw, paint, sketch, and color in the design phase. I get to write about quilting on my blog, to my friends, in this book, and I get to teach others to do what I love to do. Someday I might even enter a contest!

Have you ever lost your motivation to quilt? If so, how did you get it back?

I don't think I've ever lost the desire to quilt. There have been times in my life when other things took priority over it, though. When I get too busy with my day job, when I'm moving house, having a rough patch in my relationship, or am getting ready for a trip, then quilting might fall by the wayside. But even while those things are happening I keep thinking up new patterns and buying fabric and am staying in touch with my quilting friends because I know I will get back to it as soon as I can. I feel that it is one constant in my life, and I imagine I will quilt until I am not physically able to.

What advice would you give to a new quilter who is overwhelmed by all there is to learn about quilting?

Find a quilt shop where you feel comfortable and welcome. Take a beginner class. Pray for a good teacher. If you don't get one the first time, don't give up. Find a different teacher or a different shop.

Just learn what seems interesting to you at the time, and don't worry about what other people are doing. You are more likely to learn it if you love it, so if you want to do appliqué, do it. If you want to try art quilting then find a class or a retreat that focuses on design rather than on how to piece. There are so many different branches to quilting that it is almost impossible to learn all of them.

And you might try something and not like it at all. If that happens, it is *okay*. Just chalk it up as a learning experience, put the piece aside (UFOs—unfinished objects—are not a sin) and go on to the next thing that catches your interest. It may take you a few false starts before you find the thing that hooks you or inspires you. Just try what looks good to you and leave the rest. Think of it as an endless, all-you-can-eat buffet; just know in advance that you can never try everything, but you *can* sample a lot of things before you are full!

How would you help a new quilter tap her own creative potential?

I used to think that everyone is creative in his or her own way. However, my fiancé, Eric, says that he does not have one creative bone in his body. So for someone like him, I would say quilting is a lost cause unless you just want to replicate other people's patterns and color choices. And that's okay too—it just isn't as creative as designing from scratch, but your color choices and choice of quilting stitches will put your own unique stamp on it.

For someone who does have what I consider to be a normal amount of creativity and imagination, I would suggest just starting small—with an image, a range of colors, a shape. Meditate on it if you need to. If you are verbal, talk about it. If you are a writer, write about it. What does it resemble? What words can describe it? Now think how you can make those words into images with fabric and thread and paint or beads.

Then just try it. Don't worry about the outcome—think of it as playing with fabric the way you may have played with Play-Doh as a child. It's meant to be fun and if it stops being fun, put it aside or try something else. Don't think of it as wasted time. You learn something from every artistic experiment, even if it's just "this technique isn't for me."

Try something very small if you are truly afraid of committing to a large project. Make a postcard, or a pot holder, or a placemat—something small that you can donate to Goodwill if you really hate it. If that goes well, then next time you can make something larger until you gain confidence.

There are also books that will help you get in touch with your creative side. I've listed some in the Resources section.

Have you ever created a quilt while healing from an illness or injury? Did the process of making the quilt help you heal?

I haven't. I've been very lucky not to have any serious illnesses or injuries. And the times when I have been really sick, it's been with something like a cold or flu, and the very last thing I feel like doing then is quilting! When I injured my back, sitting was very painful, so quilting was out then too!

Have you ever made a quilt for a loved one who was sick or dying? Did it help you cope with the feelings of grief and loss?

I also haven't done this. The only person close to me who has died was my father, and at the time of his death I was also having a difficult time in my relationship. With all that was going on, I did still quilt, but not being an art quilter, I did not create anything specifically related to his death.

Have you ever made a quilt just out of sheer joy or thankfulness, or to celebrate a milestone in your life?

Not yet. I am not a very sentimental person and also I work full time, so I don't really have time to do things like this, even when it does occur to me.

Do you meditate while you quilt? Do you pray? Do you sing? Do you think positive thoughts and try to imbue the stitches with love and good energy?

I sing—a lot. I can't work without good music, especially when I get into the cutting and piecing phase. Like Alex Anderson, I dance while I'm pressing (although not so much when I'm cutting) and I need happy, upbeat music to keep me focused sometimes.

As I said earlier, I don't meditate, and I've never felt the need to pray over a quilt. If I'm making a quilt for a particular person, I do think about them a lot while I'm making it, wondering if they'll like it, choosing fabrics to suit them, that sort of thing. But that's about as far as it goes for me.

Have you ever created an heirloom to pass down to your great-great-grandchildren?

I have chosen to be child free, so this question also does not apply to me. And aside from wanting to sleep and shed on them, my cats haven't shown much interest in my quilts! I hope that my quilts will go to people who will cherish them, and I *have* given some to my friend's children and to my nieces and nephews, so they will get passed down—just not to my own offspring.

SIX

Quilting Essentials

If we are authentic—showing up to the process as who we really are, with all our biases and our strong opinions, with the things that terrify us and the visions we hold, then our creative work is our real work, the most honest and valid thing we do.

—MARY ANN TITUS

When I was growing up, there was a lot of emphasis on following rules and doing things the "correct" way. This instilled in me a fear of following my heart and doing what I loved, because I was never sure if what I loved to do would be acceptable to those in power (parents, teachers, society). As a result, any art I did produce was very ordinary and boring. My imagination was stifled—at least when it came to public expressions of creativity. I tried to fit in and suffered embarrassment any time my authentic creative side peeked out and was noticed.

It can be hard to shake this ingrained fear of striking out on your own and doing your own thing. Some people allow it to paralyze them for life. I hope that you aren't one of them! I hope that reading this book is helping you see the many ways that quilting can be an asset in your life. And most of all, I hope that hearing other people's stories of creativity has inspired you to express your own and follow your own path. Doing what you truly enjoy is a powerful way to center yourself. If you are worried about others' opinions, you will find it nearly impossible to relax, to feel the flow of creativity, or to settle into the bliss of the moment.

Another thing that can obscure your bliss is too many rules. When it comes to quilting, there are really only a few essential rules. Everything else is guidelines, suggestions, best practices, and opinions. In this chapter I will teach you the essential rules to start quilting. Appendix B contains a lot of nice-to-know information that can help you as you progress in skill, but if you never look at the appendix, you can still make beautiful quilts and quilted art. The beauty comes from inside you—not from a long list of "musts."

For each step along the way, I will show you how you can follow your own inclinations in the choices you make in order to create a quilt that is a true work of the heart. In some cases we will be—gasp—breaking the rules (really just breaking the "guidelines, suggestions, best practices, and opinions," and we all know what they say about opinions). But take a deep breath and relax. There are no quilting police and as long as you love the finished item, that is *all* that matters.

> I will no longer look to copy what someone else has done,
> but want to find my own voice and expand on that.
> When I finish something and "feel" it is complete in my eyes,
> it doesn't matter what kind of response I get.
> —DEBBIE KRUEGER

By now I hope you're excited about quilting; I hope you are dying to dig in and make a quilt of your own. This chapter will walk you through the steps to make a simple, pieced table runner or doll quilt. You can even add appliqué if you want. Or change it. Or add to it. This is your quilt, and you should feel free to make it your very own unique creation. Just concentrate on one step at a time, and before you know it you'll have a beautiful quilt.

If you want to jump right in, I have provided a simple pattern and instructions to make your quilt by machine, so that you can quickly see the results of your efforts. Many excellent books on traditional hand piecing and hand quilting exist and are listed in Appendix A. If you are determined to make a quilt the "old-fashioned" way, by all means give those books a look. As for me—I don't have the patience or temperament to hand piece or hand quilt! I really admire the beautiful results, but I don't think it's a skill I will ever master. For the time being, I'll describe here what I know best: machine piecing and quilting.

Basic Tools

To make a quilt, you will need some basic tools. I won't go into a deep discussion on the topic except to say to check with your local quilt shop. They will guide you in the right direction and will recommend products that will make your quilting easier and more fun.

Tools can also be broken down into two types: hardware and software. Hardware refers to the basic tools of the trade: machines, scissors, rulers, etc. Software is the fun stuff: fabrics, batting, threads, embellishments—the reason many of us started to quilt in the first place. I will also discuss a third tool, something called "wetware" in the computer industry: it refers to . . . you. Your brain. Your imagination. Your daring. Your heart. All of these things can be expressed through the creation of a quilt, and I will try to help you see where each of them can figure in along the way.

Hardware

Now I know I said I would tell you how to use your heart and imagination every step of the way, but, unfortunately, hardware is not a very imaginative topic. There are certain tools you just have to have, and aside from choosing a cute sewing machine (I personally adore my antique Singer Featherweight), there is little imagination involved. So bear with me through this section; I promise it won't be too long.

1. You will need a sewing machine that can sew both straight and zigzag stitches. Make sure it is in good working order. Have it serviced if required, and make sure it is clean and not clogged with lint. A walking foot or free-motion (or darning) foot is very useful for machine quilting. For a beginner, I'd say a walking foot is almost a necessity if you want nice, straight stitch lines and no puckers on the back of your quilt.

2. Sewing machine needles are the next necessity. Put in a new needle of the appropriate size before each project in order to avoid skipped stitches and thread breakage. There is more information about needles in Appendix B.

3. Invest in a rotary cutter, mat, and ruler. A small mat (12-by-24 inches) will do for small blocks and projects, but if you plan to become a quilter, I recommend at least a 24-by-36-inch mat or larger. There are a variety of different rotary cutters available, including ergonomic ones designed for quilters who must remain seated while cutting fabric. Rulers come in all shapes and sizes, but a 6-by-24-inch ruler is the most useful size.

4. Straight pins are used to hold strips and blocks for sewing

and also for holding on appliqué pieces for hand appliqué. The flathead kind is best, but any will do as long as they are sharp and not bent or rusted.

5. You will need an iron and ironing board. A steam iron is helpful, although not necessary. Be careful if you decide to use steam when pressing your blocks. The steam makes the fabric softer and it may lead to distorted seams and stretched bias unless you are very careful.

Small- to medium-sized safety pins are used to baste the quilt layers together before quilting. You can also do this with a long-running hand stitch or use basting spray such as Sulky Temporary Spray Adhesive or 505 Spray and Fix Fabric Adhesive on smaller pieces. I have used the Sulky adhesive on everything up to baby-quilt size and it worked well for me with the addition of safety pins in key places.

6. Small, sharp scissors to snip thread are essential. Don't use your sewing scissors for any other purpose. Keep them sharp.

That's it! Those are all the boring pieces of hardware you need. You can buy all of them at a craft store, or you can go to the quilt shop and start making lifelong friends with the staff there. That will be important, because to find really *good* quilting fabric, you have to visit a quilt shop. Discount fabric shops may seem like a bargain, but trust me on this—they aren't.

With that in mind, let's talk about the really *interesting* part of quilting—the fabrics!

Software

Now we come to the fun stuff. Software, in this instance, refers to the fabrics, batting, and threads you will use to create your quilt. Most quilters will admit that their hobby grew out of a love of fabric. Mary Ann Titus says, "I love fabric—the colors, textures, the warp and weft of it. I love how it feels in my hands. And I love the images and the feelings that arise inside when I meet a piece of fabric the likes of which I have never seen before."

Long before I started quilting, I loved fabric. I used to visit fabric shops just to fondle the material. The textures and colors and designs mesmerized me. I sewed garments, household items, and small crafts, but never thought of quilting because I had never heard of machine quilting! I thought it would all have to be done by hand and that was a daunting thought. I had a large stash of fabric, but very little of it was fit for quilting. Now, like most quilters I know, my stash grows every time I go to the quilt shop (even when I swear I'm just going for thread).

Speaking of thread, use only 100 percent cotton thread for machine piecing. Don't skimp and buy cheap thread, or your treasured quilt may fall apart. Also, do not use polyester thread, because over time it can cut through the delicate cotton fibers in your fabric. A thinner thread is better for piecing because it will allow the seams to be pressed flatter, creating neater joins.

You should choose a thread in a neutral color (gray, beige, white, or black) that blends with the fabrics you are piecing. (However, if you are sewing red to orange, you couldn't go wrong with a red or orangey-red thread. This will help you to minimize an effect that quilt show judges call "railroad tracks," where the piecing thread shows when seams on the quilt top are spread open.)

For the quilting, you may want to choose a matching or contrasting thread, or the clear or smoke nylon monofilament thread, depending on the color of your quilt top and the effect you hope to achieve. Contrasting colors will show up, while matching colors will blend in and seem to disappear. You may want to use a heavier thread for quilting if you want the design to show up, or a thinner one for a more subdued quilting design.

Thread comes in a wide variety of materials and sizes and has different uses. Delicate silk thread is often used for hand appliqué. Rayon thread is shiny and makes quilting look vibrant. Nylon monofilament thread is used when you want a quilted look but don't want the thread itself to show, such as when you're doing machine appliqué. Cotton, polyester, and polyester/cotton blends are all used for quilting and piecing, and they each come in different thicknesses. (If you are making an heirloom quilt, I would avoid using polyester threads for piecing, as they can cut through the cotton fabric over time, causing seams to come apart.) Metallic and specialty threads are used mainly for embellishment.

Fabric is usually the first thing we see when we look at a quilt, and it is usually the part that quilters put the most thought (and money) into.

Purchase the best quality fabric you can afford. Expensive fabric is not necessarily good-quality fabric. Make sure that you buy from a quilt shop you trust, and learn the difference between quality fabric and the cheaper cotton on the market.

Quilters normally use 100 percent cotton fabric. There are a few different reasons for this. It washes well, it wears well, it is easy to work with, and it is strong and can withstand repeated washings.

But all 100 percent cottons are not created equal.

To determine which fabric is of better quality, inspect the weave closely. A tighter weave allows less light through and usually indicates a higher-quality material.

When fabric companies begin printing a new design, they do a test run to ensure that the colors are correct and that the pattern elements are properly aligned. To do this, they usually use lower-quality muslin than they will use for their later runs. These early runs look identical to the later runs, and often the only discernable difference is in the feel (or the hand) of the fabric. (Hand refers to the tactile feel of the fabric. If it feels flimsy or thin it is probably not a good candidate for quilting. Sizing is added to the thinner fabrics so they will feel like higher-quality fabrics, so beware of stiff fabrics that are made up of more sizing than threads.)

These poorer-quality runs are usually sold to discount fabric stores, so chances are if one shop is charging ten dollars a yard for a given fabric, and the discount store has something that looks the same for two ninety-nine, the more expensive fabric is the better quality and thus the better deal.

Thread count is important. Thin fabric will tear more easily. Cheap fabric will fade more easily, too, and the colors in a cheaper fabric may run when you wash it. I advise avoiding the discount fabric stores unless they're your only option. If you don't have a local quilt shop, go shopping on the Internet: I've listed several reputable online fabric shops in Appendix C.

Batting is the filling of the quilt sandwich. The type of batting used determines how the quilt will look once it is quilted, and also determines how warm a bed quilt or quilted garment will be.

Purchase batting that suits the quilt you are making. Depending on the intended use of your quilted item (bed quilt, wall quilt, quilted clothing, etc.), you may want to use different types of batting.

> Batting is the "filling" of your quilt sandwich. A needlepunched batting is one that has been specially designed not to pill. The woven fibers of the batting material (usually cotton, polyester, wool, or some combination) are mechanically bonded by being penetrated with barbed needles. This binds the woven materials together vertically so they are less likely to come apart. Loft refers to the thickness or fluffiness of the batting.

Batting comes in different lofts and is made of different materials. The most common types are 100 percent cotton, polyester/cotton blends, and polyester. There is also 100 percent silk batting, which is extremely soft and light. It is used for quilted garments and for bed quilts in warm climates. You can also find black batting for use on dark-colored quilts. (This will prevent bearding, when fibers of batting poke through the fabric.) Wool batting is another option, but it tends to beard more than other types, even when bonded or needlepunched, and is also more susceptible to moth damage.

How to Make a (Very) Basic Quilt

Before we get into the nitty-gritty, how-to stuff, I want to give you a little bit of background on choosing and preparing your fabric. After that, we'll learn how to cut using a rotary cutter and mat, and then how to chain piece, press, and assemble the blocks. We will then choose a simple quilting pattern that you can execute by hand or machine. Finally, we'll bind and label your creation.

Please feel free to diverge from my instructions. What makes quilting exciting for me and other quilters is "doing our own thing."

Choose colors and fabrics that you love. If you are scared of color, you're not alone, and we'll address that in the section called Design Choices.

Design a unique and personalized label. After all, you want your masterpiece to be recognizable as yours to your heirs and art collectors many years from now! Add some beading—just a little can add sparkle and pizzazz. Paint a picture on your quilt or incorporate pictures your children or grandchildren have drawn. Create your own appliqué pattern. Do whatever you want to make this quilt your own special creation. Remember: there is no "wrong" way to make a quilt. Whatever makes your heart sing and thrills you is the right thing for you and for your quilt.

Now let's get started . . .

Design Choices

The overall effect of your quilt will depend largely on your choices of fabric colors, texture, and values. Don't let those terms scare you. Design theory can be boiled down to really quite simple guidelines about *color*, *texture*, and *value.*

Color is usually the first thing we notice about a quilt. Our eyes are naturally drawn to bright, pretty objects, and we may like a quilt initially because it uses our favorite colors. But a wall could be painted your favorite color, too, and you wouldn't necessarily give it any awards.

Next we may notice the shapes of the pattern itself. Is it a very regular block pattern? Ad hoc? Curvy and organic? We may notice the visual texture of the fabrics. Are they densely patterned florals? Are they quirky geometrics? Are they gentle tone-on-tones? We may like any or all of the textural elements of the quilt, but even that's not always enough to hold our interest. You can look at floral wallpaper and not be intrigued. You can look at the pattern of ceramic tiles on your floor and not be swept away. So texture and shape, although important, are not the reasons we love a given quilt.

In order for a piece of art—whether a painting or novel, a sculpture or a quilt—to catch our eye, it must offer something more than the sum of its parts. It must keep the eye *and* the mind interested. We must continually discover new things about it. In a novel, this would mean finding hidden layers of meaning. In a sculpture, it would be noticing how skillfully the artist created a lifelike figure out of marble or clay. In a painting, it would mean examining how the artist used tricks of light and shadow to draw the eye around the painting, to highlight different parts of the scene and draw our attention to the important bits.

A quilt is very much like a painting. It uses color and texture and, in order to be interesting, it must use contrast. Contrast (or *value* as it is called in quilting) is the "tricks of light and shadow." Without contrasting values in your quilt, it will appear flat and dull. No matter how vibrant the color scheme, or complicated the patchwork, if the quilt does not use different values of fabrics, it will be lifeless and dull.

Value

Value refers to the relative lightness or darkness of a fabric, as compared to black or white. A fabric that appears to have a dark value when placed next to a lighter fabric could also be a light, if it were in turn placed next to an even darker fabric. For example, in Figure 1, the gray on the left has a darker value than the gray on the right.

Figure 1

In Figure 2, however, we can see that adding the black square has suddenly turned our dark gray into a medium.

Figure 2

The importance of value can best be demonstrated by comparing two quilt blocks.

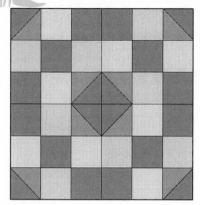 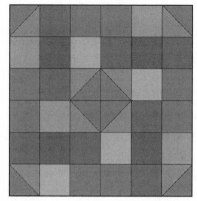

Figure 3   Figure 4

Figure 3 makes good use of value. The varying values draw the eye around the quilt the way the painter draws our eye around the painting. The block seems to sparkle and we are kept interested.

Figure 4, while it contains pretty colors, does not do a good job of holding our interest. The similarity in value of the various fabrics makes the block very dull and lifeless. It does not have the same "pop" as Figure 3. Although analogous color schemes can look dramatic and subdued, this one doesn't work, because the fabrics are all too similar in value.

Color

Although color is an integral element of quilt design, it is not the most important element. When deciding what fabric to put where, you should always look first at its *value*. That said, color is still the element most people notice first, and it is the one element of fabric that first attracts me. To make a quilt you love, start with colors you love. If you are having problems with the technical aspects of quilting, working with fabrics you adore will help get you through the rough patches.

Color theory can seem daunting if you've never taken an art class. There are all sorts of specialized terms and concepts, but the essentials are pretty basic. While an in-depth study of color theory is beyond our scope, we can talk about how a good balance of warm and cool colors affects the overall look of your quilt. And, as you'll see, there is a difference between shades, tones, and tints of a color.

When choosing colors for your quilt, try to keep in mind that the overall effect should be balanced and harmonious. This can be achieved by selecting a variety of values and colors that work well together.

The block in Figure 4, for instance, uses many lovely colors, and they all have their place in a quilt. But they are all very close to the same value. They require other values along with them, and also need other colors to make the quilt more balanced and interesting.

Here's why. The colors used in Figure 4 are all cool colors; blue, green, and violet. In order for those cool fabrics to have life, they need to be placed next to a warm color.

The color wheel in Figure 5 shows the primary colors (red, yellow, and blue) as well as the secondary colors (orange, green, and violet) and the tertiary colors (yellow-green, orange-red, blue-violet, etc.). The primary colors are called primary because they are the only colors that can be combined to create other (secondary) colors. Combining the secondary col-

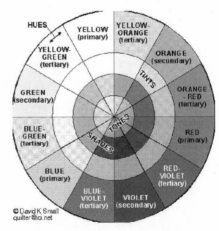

Figure 5

ors creates the tertiary colors, and so on. There are literally millions of colors—far too many to show on a single color wheel. For more details on color theory, check out my website at www. redheadedquilter.com/colortheory.

There are many ways to combine the colors you choose for your quilt. Here are the four common color palettes:

Complementary colors. These are any two colors that are opposite each other on the color wheel, such as yellow/violet, red/green, or orange/blue.

Analogous colors. These are any colors that are adjacent to each other on the color wheel, such as blue-green, green, and yellow-green.

Monochromatic colors. These are shades, tints, and tones of one color, such as orange, peach, and rust. Without some variation of value and texture, monochromatic color schemes can become boring.

Triad of colors. These are colors that are an equal distance apart on the wheel, such as orange, violet, and green. For added interest, you could use three colors that are not exactly equidistant, such as violet, yellow-green, and orange.

When I am selecting colors for a quilt, I often think of a landscape. If I have chosen a selection of vibrant "sunset" colors such as orange, yellow, and fuchsia, I will then choose at least one "ocean" color, like turquoise or green, to make sure that my quilt is color balanced. This gives the quilt some cool areas for the eye to rest, and keeps the warm colors from overwhelming the viewer.

Finally, keep these three thoughts in mind when selecting your colors:

1. Every quilt can benefit from the addition of tones. These sub-

dued colors give the eye a place to rest. Tones are the combination of primary colors with gray. For example, dusty rose is a tone of red.

2. If you choose the right values in your fabrics, any color combination can work, even wild color schemes.

3. Small amounts of bright, warm colors will give your quilt sparkle, while small amounts of cool colors will add shadows and increase the overall vibrancy of your quilt.

Texture

The third important design concept is visual texture. This refers to the visual feel of the fabric. Does the pattern look smooth or rough? How dense is the design? Is it close together or widely spaced? Does the pattern repeat randomly, or uniformly? To create a successful design, you should include fabrics of different textures. Like contrasting values, differing textures add depth to a quilt.

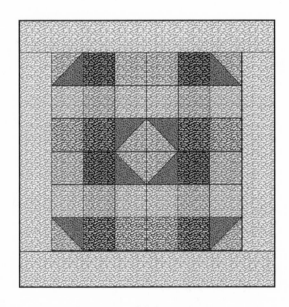

Figure 6

The quilt in Figure 6 uses fabrics that are all the same texture. This obscures the piecing and also blurs the different values.

Figure 7 is a better example of the use of different textures. (I'm not saying it's a beautiful quilt, just that the differing textures give it more life and sparkle.)

Figure 7

When creating a quilt, you should always vary at least two of the three design elements, color, value, or texture. For example, if your quilt is made of all blue fabrics, make sure that you use different values of blue and fabrics with different visual textures. If your quilt is made of all very light or dark fabrics, make sure to use different textures and colors. This will keep the eye moving around the quilt and will keep viewers interested as they discover new dimensions in the design.

SEVEN

Let's Quilt!

There are two kinds of people,
those who finish what they start and so on.

—ROBERT BYRNE

Okay, enough theory, let's get to the fun part: I've designed a quilt for you. It is a *very* simple pieced block. I designed this block using a computer program called Electric Quilt. You can purchase the latest version from electricquilt.com. You can also use a pencil and paper to design blocks.

I designed this block myself, so the usual copyright notices apply. If you take classes from any reputable teacher, you will have to buy the book or pattern that he or she is teaching from, since it's not legal for them to make money using someone else's patterns without paying for them. For the purposes of this lesson, please don't sell my pattern, or any item (quilted or otherwise) with my pattern on it. You can make copies of it for your own personal use if you would like.

The block is a traditional block called the Hourglass. If you look at it with your head tilted to the side, you'll see why. It is a relatively complex block—not complicated to make, but complex in terms of the color values. To make this block, you'll need to select five different color values: a dark, a medium dark, a medium, a light medium, and a light. Don't worry; it's not as hard as it sounds. Look at the diagram below to see what I mean. I have given some suggestions for colors, but you can certainly choose your own.

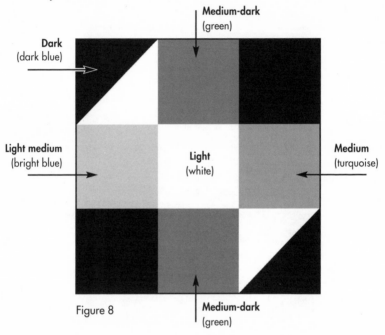

Figure 8

If you are having trouble determining the value of fabrics you want to use, photocopy the fabrics. This will make them appear in gray scale and will let you more easily see which fabrics are a particular value. Sometimes you'll be surprised at which fabrics turn out to be light or dark!

The actual colors are not important at this stage, but you should choose colors you like and that go together well, keeping in mind the discussion of color in the theory section of this chapter. We will assemble four of these blocks to make our quilt.

How Much Fabric Will I Need?

In order to determine how much fabric you'll need for a given quilt, you will need to know how large the finished quilt will be, as well as how many shapes (squares, half-square triangles, etc.) will be in the quilt, and how many of each of those shapes you will need.

For this example, I have determined that I will need twenty-eight solid blocks and eight half-square triangles. My experience tells me that this will not require very much fabric, and if I were setting out to purchase new fabric, I would buy one fat quarter of each color, plus another fat quarter (or perhaps a half a yard) to complete the borders and bindings. I would likely choose my backing from a coordinating fabric, buying a piece of fabric equal to the dimensions of the quilt, plus two inches on all sides. (Keep in mind that fabric will shrink when you wash it, so always buy slightly more than you need.)

> A fat quarter is a quarter yard of fabric cut eighteen by twenty-two inches. It is cut this way rather than from the full width of the fabric bolt in order to give the quilter a larger piece of usable fabric.

In reality, I would likely just draw fabric from my stash and I might even buy extra on purpose so I'll have leftovers.

To be more precise, I will require the following amounts of fabric to make four nine-inch Hourglass blocks, and a one-inch lapped border. My border is made from my medium fabric. These amounts will complete your quilt top. You will need additional amounts for the backing and binding. As you can see, the yardage required will make more blocks than we need in some cases. You can save this fabric for another use, or create additional quilt blocks to enlarge your wall quilt.

Value	Total Yardage Required	# of finished blocks this will make	# of blocks needed
Light	1/4 yard	22	12
Light Medium	1/8 yard	11	4
Medium (blocks)	1/8 yard	11	4
Medium (border)	1/2 yard	N/A	N/A
Medium Dark	1/8 yard	11	8
Dark	1/4 yard	22	16

Preparing Your Fabric

In order to prepare your fabric for quilting, you should wash it with a mild detergent such as Synthrapol for hand-dyed fabrics, or Retayne for commercial fabrics. Synthrapol washes out excess dye, which can stain other fabrics, and also keeps it from redepositing on other fabrics washed at the same time. Retayne sets the colors in commercially made fabrics and thus helps keep them from running onto your other fabrics. Both can be purchased on the Internet or from quilting shops.

Another option is to wash the fabric using a Shout Color Catcher sheet. They look similar to fabric softener sheets, but they actually pull loose dye out of the wash water so that it won't redeposit on the fabric. These are the best invention ever! (I even know a quilter who was so taken with the mottled appearance of her used color catcher sheets that she saved them to make a quilt out of.)

I never use fabric softener, starch, or any other additive when I wash, dry, and press my fabric. Fabric softeners will make the fabric limp and hard to work with, and will also prevent temporary adhesives like those found on fusible appliqué products from sticking. Fabric softener sheets can leave greasy spots on fabric. Starch is sometimes recommended when you are using fabric of lesser quality that may be too limp to work with easily. (If you do use starch, make sure to wash it out completely when the quilt is finished. Many insects like to eat starch and will eat your quilt if you leave starch in the fabric; I just avoid it entirely.)

After washing your fabric, dry it in the dryer until it is almost dry, then quickly remove it and press it gently with a hot iron to remove any wrinkles. If you are not going to use it immediately, you can fold it and store it somewhere dry, away from light and away from any drafts that might blow dust onto it. Never use a closed plastic container for long-term storage! They can trap moisture and mildew your fabrics, ruining them.

If you find that the threads on the edges of your fabrics unravel during washing and drying, try cutting a small triangle off each corner of the fabric before washing. This will help keep the threads from unraveling. Alternately, if you have a serger, you can serge around the edges, or sim-

> A serger is like a sewing machine. It sews over the raw edges of the cloth and creates a smooth seam that won't unravel. Most knit garments have serged seams.

ply zigzag with your machine. Unraveling occurs most often with loosely woven fabrics, but can affect even tight weaves.

Cutting your Fabric Strips

There are four basic steps to cutting strips from your prepared fabric:

1. Fold the fabric in half, selvages together. If you are using a fat quarter, match the selvage edge with the cut edge, making sure that the fold is on the grain of the fabric. How do you do that? Easy—fold the fabric and hold it up. Let the fold hang

free. If it is not perfectly folded on its own, slide one edge of the fabric either left or right to straighten out the fold. The fold line should fall on the straight of grain. If the edges don't match up, it doesn't matter, but folding on the grain is very important.

2. Carefully put the fabric on your rotary cutting mat, aligning the fold with a horizontal line on your mat. Place a six-by-twenty-four-inch ruler at right angles to the fold, aligning a horizontal line on the ruler with the fold of the fabric. Put the ruler close to the raw edge of the fabric. If you are right-handed, put it near the right-hand edge (vice versa for left-handed quilters). Hold the ruler firmly so that it does not slip or wobble and be very careful of your fingers. Begin cutting—away from your body—with your rotary cutter. Stop when the blade is just past your hand.

3. Without moving the blade or the ruler, walk your fingers up the ruler and hold it firmly again. Continue cutting and walking your hand in this manner until you have removed the raw edge.

4. Once the raw edge is removed, either walk to the other side of your cutting surface, or turn the mat around without disturbing the fabric. Place the ruler on the newly cut edge, aligning a vertical line on the ruler with the cut edge of the fabric, and a horizontal line on the ruler with the folded edge of the fabric. Use the measurements on the ruler to cut the width of fabric that you want, using the same "cut and walk" method as in step 3.

For our example, we are making blocks that finish to nine inches. Each piece of the block will finish to three-by-three inches and will have a quarter-inch seam allowance all around. With this in mind, our strips must be cut to three and a half inches wide.

To get the plain squares that we need, lay the strip from which you want to cut the squares along a horizontal line on your cutting mat. Use your ruler to cut off the selvage and square up the end, then measure in three and a half inches from that cut edge, being careful to align the ruler with the other two cut edges of your fabric. Use the rotary cutter to cut the strip into the required number of squares.

In order to determine how many strips you need to cut, you can either do the calculations manually or use a preprinted guide like *The Quilter's Pocket Reference*. This little booklet contains all the most common calculations used by quilters and was the source of the information below and for some of the information in the table above.

For example, if you are cutting squares that will finish to three inches, such as in this example, a quarter yard of fabric will yield twenty-two three-inch finished squares. The table lists how many blocks can be cut from each amount of purchased yardage.

To calculate this manually, follow the directions below, excerpted from *The Quilter's Pocket Reference*.

Step One: Add one-half inch to the desired finished length to get the cut length.

Step Two: Divide the usable fabric width (forty inches) by the cut length. Round the answer down to a whole number. This tells you how many squares can be cut from one strip between selvages. (Quilting cotton is normally about forty-five inches wide, but it will shrink when you wash it, so assuming forty usable inches is generally a safe bet.)

Step Three: Divide the total number of squares needed by the number of squares per strip. Round the answer up to a whole number. This tells you how many strips you need.

Step Four: Multiply the number of strips needed by the cut length. This tells you how many inches of fabric you need.

Step Five: Convert the inches to yards; always add extra yardage (at least one-quarter yard) for safety.

Cutting Your Fabric Triangles

Our block also uses half-square triangles. There are a few methods for making them, including commercially available products such as Thangles. I'm going to show you how to use the grid method, which is a little time consuming but almost foolproof for new quilters.

The grid method allows you to make many half-square triangles without sewing on the bias. This lessens the chance that you will accidentally stretch the fabric.

1. Cut equal-sized squares or rectangles of your two fabrics (for this block, that means your light and your dark) using your rotary mat and ruler. Make them large enough to get the required number of half-square triangles out of them. For example, Figure 9 was cut seven inches by seven inches in order to accommodate two three-and-a-half-inch squares across and two down.

2. Place the fabrics right sides together, carefully aligning the edges. You can pin them together if you need to, to keep them from sliding.

3. Using a mechanical pencil, lightly draw a grid on the lighter fabric, making the squares of the grid three and a half inches. These lines will be in the seam allowance and won't show.

4. Draw diagonal lines through the sections of the grid, as in the illustration below. You will eventually cut on this line, so this marking won't show either.

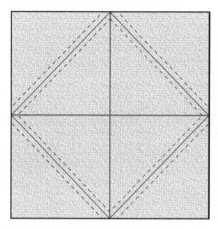

Figure 9

5. Draw lines one-quarter inch from each side of the diagonal lines. (There are special tools to help you do this, but you can also just align the one-quarter-inch line of your ruler with the drawn line, and then draw along the edge of the ruler.) These will be your sewing lines. If you're in a rush and don't want to draw in the sewing lines, use a $1/4$-inch foot and sew no more than a scant one-quarter inch from the diagonal lines. You can do this without lifting the presser foot if you follow the sewing lines around the grid. Use a short stitch length.

6. Cut the squares apart on all your grid lines, and then cut them apart again on all your diagonal lines. You should be left with several half-square triangles that measure exactly three-and-a-half inches by three-and-a-half inches. Carefully press them open with the seam allowance toward the darker fabric. Use the tip of your iron and be careful not to stretch them.

Assembling Your blocks

Now that you have your squares and half-square triangles made, it's time to assemble your block. Refer to the diagram below and lay out your pieces until you are happy with the look of the block. Lay out all four blocks before you start to piece them (you'll see why in a moment).

Figure 10

One piecing method, which simplifies things, is called Chain Piecing. This is the method I'll describe here. We will sew two patches together at a time, and then sew on the third patch of each row. Once all our rows are sewn and pressed, we'll assemble them into our quilt blocks.

The top rows of your blocks consist of one half-square triangle, one medium-dark square, and one dark square.

Being careful with the alignment, sew a half-square triangle to a medium-dark square with a one-quarter-inch seam. Without breaking your thread, sew the next half-square triangle to a medium-dark square. Repeat this with four half-square triangles. This will create the upper left-hand corner of all four of your blocks.

The second row consists of a light-medium, a light, and a medium. Without breaking your thread, sew all four light-mediums to the light squares.

The third row consists of a dark, a medium-dark, and a half-square triangle. Without breaking your thread, sew all four darks to medium-darks.

Cut the hanging chain off the machine and start again at the beginning, this time sewing the last square in the row to the other two. Make sure you get them in the correct order and alignment and sew the third block onto each row.

Once all the rows are completed, lay them out to form the blocks. Do not sew them together yet, but just lay them out on a table or design board to make sure that all the blocks and rows are in the correct order and that they are all the same length.

If you are satisfied with the order of the blocks, press the seams on the top and bottom rows outward. Press the seams on the middle rows inward. This will help with aligning the seams when you put the blocks together.

To complete your blocks, attach the top row to the middle row, carefully lining up the seams. We have pressed the seams so that they will butt together. Gently wiggle the butted seams into place with your fingertips. Pinning at this point would throw the seams out of alignment, so once both seams are matched, sew a careful one-quarter-inch seam, holding the intersections by hand as you sew. Sew the bottom row onto the middle row in the same manner. Repeat this with all the remaining blocks. Press the blocks.

You must check the block to ensure that each corner squares up. If each corner is ninety degrees, you are ready to piece the quilt top together. If not, follow the instructions below.

Squaring Up a Block

Before squaring up your blocks, finish piecing all the blocks. Measure them carefully and use the smallest measurement as your guide. If there is less than one-eighth-inch difference in the size of the blocks, they may not require squaring. But if the difference is more than one-eighth of an inch, follow the instructions below:

Press the block carefully with a warm, dry iron until it is flat.

Place the block on your rotary cutting mat and place a square ruler (larger than your block) close to the top-right corner of the block (about one-eighth of an inch or less from the edge). Use a horizontal and vertical line on your ruler to line up with a horizontal and a vertical seam on your block. Use your rotary cutter to carefully slice off the right and top edges, creating a perfectly squared corner.

Turn the block one hundred eighty degrees, so that the opposite (untrimmed) corner is now on the top right. Line up a horizontal and a vertical line on your ruler with the square corner you just cut, making sure that your ruler is covering nine and a half inches of your block in each direction. (The "extra" half inch on this nine-inch block is your seam allowance.)

Trim the other sides of the block carefully. You should now have a perfectly square block. Measure it and make sure that you cut all other blocks square and to this size. They may be slightly less than nine inches square; if that's the case, it's okay, as long as all four blocks are exactly the same size.

Piecing the Quilt Top

You're almost finished!

Use the pressed seams on the edges of your blocks to butt the seams together and stitch first the two top blocks, then the two bottom blocks together.

Align the seams once again and stitch the top row to the bottom. Press the seams flat, if necessary.

You are now ready to square up your quilt top in preparation for applying borders.

Squaring Up the Quilt

Before applying any type of border, you must measure your quilt top to ensure that it is square. This does not mean that you cannot have a rectangular quilt; rather it means that each of your four corners must form a perfect ninety-degree angle. You square up a quilt top the same way you squared up your individual blocks.

First, measure your quilt across the top, middle, and bottom. Write down these three measurements. They should all be the same. . . but seldom are, especially for a new quilter.

Next measure your quilt top to bottom along the left side, middle, and right sides, and write down these measurements. They should also all be the same.

If the measurements for the width or height of your quilt are all within a half an inch of each other, you can probably hide the small discrepancy when you apply the border. However, if the measurements differ by more than a half inch, if you plan to enter the quilt in any sort of competition, or if knowing that the quilt top is uneven will bother you, you will have to square up the top so that all four corners are perfect right angles.

To do this, make sure your quilt top is pressed flat with a warm, dry iron, and then lay it on the largest cutting mat you own. If the quilt is larger than the mat (which is usually the case), lay it flat on a table with the cutting mat under one corner of the quilt. Use your rotary ruler or the lines on the mat to check that each corner is square. If not, sliver trim them as you did the blocks, being careful not to take too much off any one corner. Repeat the process with the other three corners.

Measure the quilt again and make sure that your measurements all match. Now you are ready to apply the borders.

Borders

Borders frame the central portion of the quilt. Not all quilts use borders, but if you want to put one on yours, there are three main types of borders you can apply to your quilt—lapped, mitered, or pieced. You can use just one border or any combination of these borders and can make them any size you like. For our example, we will make a one-inch-wide, lapped border.

Applying a Lapped Border

We will apply the top and bottom borders first and then the side borders.

To determine how long the first two border pieces must be, measure across the center of the quilt from side to side. Cut two fabric strips this long and as wide as your border width, plus seam allowance. Assuming that all our measurements have been perfect up until now, you will need two nineteen-inch-long strips that are each one and a half inches wide (to account for seam allowances). If your quilt is not exactly nineteen inches wide, use whatever width it actually is.

Fold the border strip in half lengthwise, and put a light crease in the middle with your iron, or put a straight pin there to mark the center. Do the same with the other border strip.

Line up the marked middle of the border strip with the middle of your quilt top and pin it in place, right sides together.

1. Pin each end of the border strip to the quilt top, matching up the raw edge of the border strip with the raw edge of the quilt top.

2. Pin in between the edge and the center, gently easing in any excess bulk.

3. Sew the borders on with a quarter-inch seam allowance.

4. Press the borders outward.

5. Repeat the above steps to make the side borders for the quilt top. Make sure to measure the new borders in addition to the body of the quilt. Assuming that all your cutting and piecing has been perfect, the measurement should be twenty-one and a half inches (nineteen inches for the quilt body, plus three inches for the border strips you have added).

6. After attaching the side borders, as in steps one through three, press those as well. Your quilt top is now completed!

Honestly, this is where I usually quit. For me, it's like assembling a jigsaw puzzle. Once the top is done, I'm happy. However, for those of you who enjoy finishing projects, or who want to know how to quilt and bind your quilt top, read on.

Preparing Your Top for Quilting

Even very small quilts like our sample must be basted before they are quilted. Basting your quilt is a very important step. If it's not done carefully, the backing may pucker or the top may become distorted or crooked as you quilt.

There are three layers to a quilt: the backing, the batting, and the quilt top. Basting connects these three layers so that you may quilt the item without worrying about the distortions mentioned above. There are several ways to baste a quilt. For a small one like ours, I would use basting spray. If you are sensitive to chemicals or just don't want to use the spray, you can also baste with safety pins or thread.

Always begin with batting and backing slightly larger than your quilt top. This is necessary because as you quilt the project, it will take up some of this slack. This is especially true for items that are quilted in a small, all-over pattern such as stippling.

For small projects (thirty inches and under), the batting and backing should be about two inches larger than the quilt top on all sides. For large quilts, or projects that you know will be heavily quilted, allow at least four inches on all sides.

Basting with Basting Spray

Basting sprays are spray adhesives designed not to harm the fabrics. Most brands simply wash out when the quilt is washed. Others evaporate over time. Some brands are toxic if inhaled (and are labeled as such).

If you suffer from allergies or asthma, or have pets or small children in the house, I recommend using a nontoxic brand such as Sulky's KK 2000 Temporary Spray Adhesive. This product is nonflammable, nontoxic, and ozone friendly. The label claims that it is also odorless, and while it does not have much smell, I would hardly call it odorless. I've used this product for many small projects and have found that the bond holds well for up to several weeks at a time, if not disturbed.

You should follow the instructions on the can if you choose to use a basting spray, but general instructions are included here for reference.

Ensure that the backing fabric and batting have been properly prepared (fabric should washed, dried, pressed, and cut to size, and batting should be unfolded and left to rest for several hours to relax fold lines).

Spread the batting on a flat surface, protected with an old bedsheet or a scrap of muslin. Apply the spray to the batting, in a light, even mist, following manufacturer's instructions.

Spread the backing fabric, right side up, onto the sprayed batting. Gently smooth the fabric from the center outwards, removing any wrinkles or tucks. You may peel off the fabric and reposition it if necessary.

Turn the project over and repeat the process with the quilt top, being careful to align all the cut edges properly.

Basting with Safety Pins

Most machine-quilted projects are basted with safety pins. There are even pre-bent safety pins designed specifically for basting quilts. The pointed part of the pin is bent in the middle to make it easier to close when it is in a flat surface. They can be purchased at quilt supply shops and some department and craft stores. Ordinary safety pins work equally well, but are more difficult to close.

1. In order to pin baste a quilt find a clean flat surface that is larger than your quilt. A kitchen table works well, although you will have to be very careful not to mar the finish on the table with the safety pins.

2. Ensure that the backing fabric and batting have been properly prepared (see above).

3. Spread the backing *right* side down on the table, smoothing it

carefully. Tape the edges down with masking tape, starting with the top and bottom then left and right sides, then the opposing corners. If the quilt is large, you may need to add more tape between the pieces already in place. Always make sure the fabric is pulled smooth by the tape and that you tape opposite sides to provide equal tension on the fabric.

4. Spread the batting on top of the backing, smoothing it out carefully so that there are no ripples or folds.

5. Spread the quilt top, *right* side up, on the batting. The batting and backing should extend from two to four inches around all sides of the quilt top.

6. Begin pinning in the center of the quilt, being careful not to pin across any future quilting lines. Pins should be placed no more than three inches apart in any direction. A good way to estimate this distance is to put your fist on the quilt. There should be a pin at all four corners of your fist.

7. Continue pinning from the center outward until the entire quilt top is secured to the backing.

Quilting

After your quilt top is pieced, the top squared up, the borders attached, and the basting done, the next step is to decide how you want to quilt it. The method you choose will determine what you do next. This section will describe each method and then give detailed instructions on how to accomplish each.

Machine Quilting

Machine quilting does not normally use a quilt frame the way that traditional hand quilting does. Instead, the quilt is basted, stabilized, and then rolled up into a manageable size before being fed into the machine. This section will provide some guidance on how to do it.

Before starting any decorative quilting, you must stabilize the quilt sandwich. To do this, select two

> While most machine quilting is not done on a frame, some is. John Flynn, an engineer turned quilter, has designed a small, easily portable quilt frame that does not require basting of the quilt. It can be used with a sewing machine, or in the traditional manner. For information, visit his website at flynnquilt.com.

or more seams that run through the center of the quilt. On our sample quilt, the stabilizing lines would be the lines between the four quilt blocks. You should quilt these lines first, and then proceed with the more detailed quilting patterns.

Handling a Large Quilt

With large pieces, it's especially helpful if you have a large surface to the left of your machine to hold the quilt up. If it sags off the table it will put strain on the sewing machine and on your hands as you try to hold it in place. If your table is too small, place another table beside it, or drape the quilt over the back of a chair.

If your quilt is quite large, you have two choices depending on the type of quilting you are about to do.

If you are going to be making straight seams, such as for stabilizing the sandwich, quilting in the ditch or channel quilting, you can roll the quilt up snugly from each side toward the middle in order to fit it into your machine. Quilt clips are handy for holding these rolled sides. Reroll the quilt and rearrange the clips as necessary to quilt the sides of the quilt. The excess length of the quilt can be folded accordion style on your lap, or draped over your shoulder.

If you are going to be doing free-motion quilting, you may want to spread the quilt out on the table (supporting it with additional tables if necessary) and "puddle" a small section of the quilt under your needle. Stitch just in that small area, then, as you move to the side of that area, leave the needle down, and carefully reposition your quilt so that you have a new puddle to quilt in.

> "Puddling" the quilt means gathering a section of quilt around your needle so that it is loose and easy to move. You don't want to drag the weight of your quilt all around while you quilt—it's tiring for you and will lead to poor stitching. Having a "puddle" of quilt gives you enough room to stitch in and prevents arm and shoulder fatigue.

To secure the beginning or ending of a line of machine quilting, you have two options.

1. If your machine is equipped with a locking stitch, you can use that, although in some cases it may leave a large knot on the back. This is not suitable for any quilt that will be entered in a show or for any quilt where the back might be seen. (I confess to doing this on a quilt that I knew would be used as a table runner, though!)

2. If your machine does not have that feature, or you do not want to use it, set the stitch length almost to zero and take two or three stitches. Gradually increase the stitch length over the course of one-quarter to one-half an inch until it is as long as you want it. When you get to the end of your stitching line, reverse the process.

Whenever possible, start and end your stitches at the edge of the quilt where the binding will cover them. If you do this, you won't have to use the short stitches because the binding stitches will cross the ends of the quilting stitches and hold them secure.

Decorative Quilting

There are a number of different ways to quilt your quilt top. The two basic methods are Machine Guided or Free Motion. Machine-guided quilting means that you quilt along straight lines, usually the piecing lines. You may quilt between pieces (known as "quilting in the ditch") or you may quilt a set distance from the seams (known as echo or outline quilting). Free-motion quilting means that you move the quilt under the sewing machine needle in a controlled fashion to create an overall pattern. You may create shapes such as stars, loops, or flowers, or you can use this method to follow a pattern traced onto the quilt top.

General Machine Quilting Guidelines

There are some general guidelines for all types of machine quilting. I always use my walking foot if I am quilting only straight and gently curving lines. This keeps all three layers moving under the needle at roughly the same speed and helps greatly in avoiding tucks and folds on the back of the quilt. For free-motion quilting, use the embroidery or free-motion foot.

1. Arrange the quilt, rolling and clipping it with quilt clips if necessary.

2. Position the starting point of your quilting beneath the needle and lower the presser foot.

3. Move the needle down and up once. (Some machines have a "needle down-up" feature that will do this with one touch of a button.)

4. As you bring the needle back up, hold the top thread and tug on it gently to bring the bobbin thread to the top of the quilt. Pull both threads back under the needle. They will be clipped later.

5. Take a few tiny securing stitches as described above. You are now ready to start quilting your quilt.

6. When you are finished quilting, clip the top thread as close as you can to the top of the quilt, being careful not to nick the fabric. Turn the quilt over and tug the bobbin thread so that the cut end of the top thread is pulled into the batting. Clip the bobbin thread.

Machine-Guided Quilting

Quilting in the Ditch

In quilting, the *ditch* is the area between any two pieced shapes in the quilt. Quilting in the ditch means running a line of stitches directly in the seam between these shapes.

Before starting this type of quilting, you should look carefully at the path you plan to take. It is best and often easier to quilt without lifting your needle, so if you can find a continuous path around your quilt top, that's the way you should go. It's not always possible, but it's the ideal situation.

Quilting in the ditch requires no marking, so if this is the only kind of quilting you plan to do, you can proceed directly to quilting.

For quilting in the ditch, it's easiest if the quilt falls down toward the needle. Some skilled quilters can simply hold the quilt up and guide it from afar. You may find it easier to lay a hand on either side of the needle and gently pull the ditch open.

Watch the area just in front of the needle, rather than the needle itself. This will help you sew a straighter stitch.

When you reach a corner, leave the needle down and lift the presser foot, then pivot the quilt, lower the presser foot, and continue sewing as before.

Echo Quilting

Echo quilting is running a line of stitches at measured intervals around a shape. This interval can be any distance you like, but is frequently one-quarter of an inch. Most sewing machines' walking feet have adjustable guides that you can set to help maintain your distance.

Echo quilting requires no marking, so if this is the only kind of quilting you plan to do, or if you plan to combine it only with in-the-ditch quilting, you can proceed to quilting.

Echo quilting is done in the same way as quilting in the ditch with the exception that the quilting itself falls one-quarter to one-half an inch from the ditch. If your walking foot does not have an echo-quilting guide, you may have to mark the line, or simply eyeball it or use the edge of your walking foot as a guide by running the edge of it along the ditch.

Channel Quilting

Channel quilting is a very simple method in which you sew a series of straight lines side by side across the quilt either horizontally or vertically. This is similar to echo quilting, in that you use the guide on your walking foot to space your stitching lines, but you generally go in a straight line rather than following the contours of a shape.

Channel quilting is done in the same way as quilting in the ditch with the exception that the quilting itself falls one-half an inch to one inch or more from the ditch. If your walking foot does not have a channel-quilting guide, you may have to eyeball it or use the edge of your walking foot as a guide by running the edge of it along the ditch.

If you want to quickly mark your quilt top for channel quilting, run strips of masking tape along where you want to quilt and quilt beside them. Be sure to remove the tape soon after quilting so that a sticky residue is not left on the fabric.

Free-Motion Quilting

Free-motion quilting means that you use your hands, rather than the machine's feed dogs, to move the quilt under the needle. This takes some practice, but in just a few hours you should be able to do a passable job at stippling, meandering (a larger version of stippling and easier to do) or creating shapes such as spirals, crescents, loops, zigzags, stars, flowers, hearts, leaves, and other shapes.

Begin your quilting as described in the General Machine Quilting Guidelines section, by putting your securing stitches in an inconspicuous spot. For free-motion quilting, run the machine very fast, and move the quilt slowly. Relax your shoulders and arms, and try to get a rhythm going. It is always a good idea to practice on a scrap quilt sandwich before attempting to quilt the real thing. Even experienced quilters usually do a "warm-up" piece before working on their quilt.

Stencil Quilting

Another form of free-motion quilting involves following a marked quilting pattern. There are thousands of different quilting stencils on the market, from the simplest curves to the most intricate motifs. There are also dozens of different methods used to transfer these stencil patterns to your quilt top. The pattern can be transferred with graphite, chalk or soapstone pencils, erasable markers, or other marking tools.

Begin your quilting as described in the General Machine Quilting Guidelines section, putting your securing stitches in an inconspicuous spot on your marked pattern. Use either the walking foot or the free-motion foot, depending on how curvy your stenciled pattern is.

Finishing Your Quilt

After the quilting is done, there are still a few steps before your quilt is complete. If you are making a wall quilt, a quilt for a show, or any quilt that you don't plan to use on a bed, you may want to add a hanging sleeve to the back. A hanging sleeve is a simple tube of fabric sewn to the back of the quilt to allow it to be hung on a rod on the wall.

The sleeve can be added before you add your binding. After the sleeve and binding are added, the last step is to create a label for your quilt. Every quilt deserves to have its history recorded and I will describe several methods for making beautiful and informative labels.

Adding a Sleeve

Any quilt that will be hung on the wall should have a sleeve. Quilt show organizers usually require sleeves as well—for ease of hanging—and they specify the size it must be. A properly applied sleeve will support the weight of the quilt evenly so that it may hang for long periods of time with little stress on the delicate pieced top.

The best time to add the sleeve is before adding the binding. This method allows you to machine stitch the sleeve to the quilt. This makes it stronger and is much faster than adding it totally by hand.

Your sleeve can be made of the same fabric as the back of your quilt (preferred), or it can be plain muslin or some coordinating fabric. The instructions below have been adapted from *Celtic Quilts: A New Look for Ancient Designs*.

To create a four-inch-wide sleeve

1. Cut a piece of fabric nine inches wide and as long as the width of your quilt.

2. On the short ends of this strip, turn under and press a three-eighths-of-an-inch hem. Turn under and press again, then topstitch the hems in place.

3. Fold the strip in half, right side out. Align the raw edges and press the fold. Pin the sleeve to the back of your quilt, matching the raw edges of the sleeve with the top raw edge of your quilt. Make sure that the sleeve is approximately three-quarters of an inch narrower than the width of your quilt.

4. Using a scant quarter-inch seam, machine stitch the top edge of the sleeve to the quilt. Your binding will cover this seam.

5. Hand stitch the bottom of the sleeve to the back of the quilt, being careful not to sew through the front of the quilt.

Creating and Adding the Binding

Many quilting books describe how to create a bias binding. A bias binding will be more flexible and can go around scalloped or otherwise uneven edges. This method is time consuming and often confusing for a new quilter, so I will describe a simpler method that is just as effective.

Straight-edged quilts do not require a bias binding. Since most fabrics are not exactly on grain, you can usually just cut your binding strips from selvage to selvage. When these strips are folded, the threads will be slightly off grain, giving a similar effect to a bias binding, but without all the tedious sewing and cutting. The following instructions are adapted from *Celtic Quilts: A New Look at Ancient Designs*.

To determine how many strips to cut, measure the length times two and width times two of your quilt. Add these together to get its perimeter. Divide this number by the useable width of your binding fabric to get the number of strips you will need to cut.

To make a narrow binding, cut two-and-a-half-inch-wide binding strips. If you prefer a wider binding, add another half inch to an inch to this measurement. Cut the number of strips you determined in step one. Piece the strips together with a diagonal seam, pressing the seam allowance open.

Fold the binding strips wrong sides together and press, carefully aligning the raw edges.

Open the binding strip at one end and fold the lower corner inward, creating a forty-five-degree angle. Cut away the tip of the triangle that is formed inside the binding, leaving a quarter-inch seam allowance. Refold the binding strip. This is shown in the figure below.

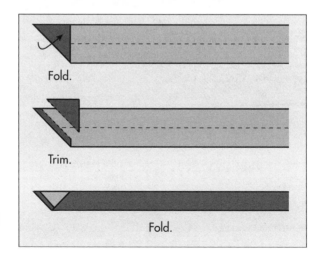

Figure 11

Fold.

Trim.

Fold.

To ensure that your binding is long enough, test it by laying it around the perimeter of the quilt. Make sure that the seams in the binding do not fall on the corners of the quilt and that the binding is at least five inches longer than the perimeter of the quilt. If it is not long enough, piece on another strip and press it as described above.

Choose an inconspicuous spot along the edge of the quilt to start your binding. Lay the raw edge of the binding strip along the raw edge of the quilt, leaving the first five inches unsewn for now. Pin the binding in place if necessary. Using your walking foot, stitch the binding to the quilt using a three-eighths-of-an-inch seam allowance.

Stop sewing three-eighths of an inch from the first corner with your needle down. Pivot the quilt and stitch straight off the corner at a forty-five-degree angle as shown in the figure below.

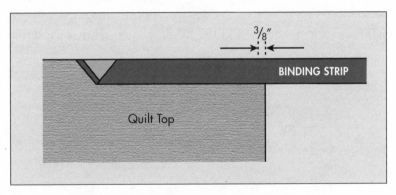

Figure 12

Lift the needle and remove the quilt from under the presser foot. Fold the binding strip up and away from the corner at a forty-five-degree angle, and then fold it back down on itself, even with the adjacent edge. Make sure that the resulting pleat is straight and even with the edge of the quilt. This is shown in figure 13.

Holding the thread out of the way, slide the corner of the quilt back under the presser foot and begin sewing right at the edge of the quilt as shown in the figure below.

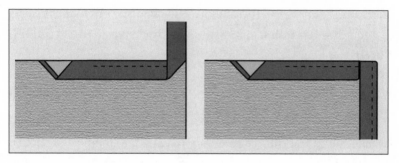

Figure 13

Continue around the quilt, completing each corner like the first. Stop sewing several inches before reaching the binding's starting point. Keep the needle and presser foot down.
Open the fold at the beginning of the binding and slide the end of the binding inside. Trim away the excess binding, leaving at least a one-inch overlap. Tuck the cut end back inside the fold so that no cut edges are exposed, and finish sewing the binding seam as shown in the figure below.

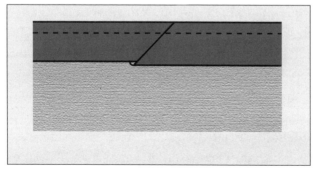

Figure 14

Turn the folded edge of the binding to the back of the quilt and stitch in place by hand, being careful not to sew through the front of the quilt. The folded edge of the binding should cover the initial machine stitching. When turning the corners, clip a small triangle off the corner of the quilt sandwich. This will make it easier to get a nice flat miter. Hand stitch the tucked end of the binding closed.

Creating the Label

Labels serve three main audiences:

1. They help the quilter remember when she made a particular quilt. Believe me, this is not as silly as it sounds. After you've been quilting for just a couple of years and have a pile of completed quilts, you will appreciate this small bit of record keeping.

2. The second audience to appreciate quilt labels is anyone who views the quilt in your home, the home of the recipient (if it is a gift), or in a show or gallery. Everyone knows who painted the Mona Lisa, and everyone should know who created your masterpiece. In quilt shows, properly detailed labels are a requirement.

3. The third audience for quilt labels may not yet be born. These are your children, grandchildren, all your descendants, and future historians and quilt lovers. Several states, including Michigan, now have quilt history projects seeking to find and preserve as many quilts as they can. They are taking oral histories from the makers of these quilts when possible and are gathering as much documentation as possible. This art form is widely appreciated and admired, and adding a label to every quilt you make will let your name and accomplishments live on in history.

What information must I include? The minimum information you should include on a quilt label is the title of the quilt, maker's name(s), designer's name (if not the same person), the date you completed the quilt, and your geographic location. Other good information to include is your age when you made it, any special fabrics or techniques used, any original patterns used, and your inspiration for the quilt. If the quilt is a gift, include the occasion for which it was made and the recipient's name, age, and location.

What kinds of labels can I make? Labels are usually created on muslin or other light-colored fabric and then hand stitched to the back of the quilt. You can use many tools to write your labels, including indelible markers such as Pigma Micron markers, fabric crayons, and embroidered or machine-stitched lettering. You can make the label yourself from fabric or use iron-on transfer labels or computer-printed labels. Each of these methods will be discussed.

"Homemade" Labels

The most common type of label is homemade. These labels are simply pieces of muslin with handwritten information and, sometimes, simple drawings. To create a homemade label, you will need the following tools and supplies:

1. Scrap of muslin, one-half to one inch larger all around than your finished label

2. Pigma Micron or other indelible markers, or fabric crayons

3. Freezer paper

4. Scissors

5. Iron

6. Thread to attach label to quilt back

Cut the muslin in the shape you want your label to be, leaving a half-inch to one-inch border all around. This will be turned under before sewing the label to the quilt.

Press the back of the label onto the shiny side of a piece of freezer paper, being careful not to get wax on your iron. (Use a pressing cloth, if necessary.) This will stiffen the label and make it easier to write and draw on it.

Turn the label over and use the markers to write the information you want on your label. You may also draw or trace pictures onto the label and color them in. When you are done writing and drawing the label, peel the freezer paper off the back.

Lightly press under a half-inch to one-inch hem all around the label, and then hand stitch it in place on the back of the quilt. Labels are usually placed in the lower right side, but this is not a hard-and-fast rule.

Iron-On Transfer Labels

This kind of label can be purchased in a book such as *Iron-On Transfers for Quilt Labels.* The labels in this book are printed in reverse mirror image so that when you iron them onto your label fabric they appear the right way around. You can use your fabric markers and crayons, embroidery, buttons, and other embellishments to decorate the label. This book contains fifty-one different labels for all occasions. Detailed instructions for this method may be found in the book, but, as above, it's a good idea to iron the label onto freezer paper before trying to write on it or color it in.

Computer Printed Labels

There are two ways to print labels on fabric using your computer.

One is to purchase a product such as June Tailor's Washable Colorfast Printer Fabric. Sold in packages of three eight-and-a-half by eleven-inch sheets for about $12.99, this specially treated fabric can be fed into an ink-jet or bubble-jet printer. The result is a colorfast image of your photo or text that can be used either as a label or as a quilt block. This product can be washed, though some fading may occur. If you know that the quilt will not be washed, you can use June Tailor's Dry Clean Only version of printable fabric. This product is slightly cheaper, at around $8.25 for four sheets. More information can be found at junetailor.com.

The other method is to buy a product such as Bubble Jet Set. This is a chemical solution that you can use to treat cotton or silk. One thirty-eight-ounce bottle costs around $8.50 and will make about thirty-two treated sheets.

These and many other computer-related quilting items can be found at compuquilt.com.

Unique Labels

A book like *One-of-a-Kind Quilt Labels: Unique Ideas for a Special Finishing Touch,* by Thea Nerud, offers many great ideas for creating fun labels. Thea tells you how to make everything from a fabric envelope to photo labels to a label that looks like a tiny car coming out of a garage.

Adding a custom label is a great way to personalize your quilt. After all the hours and effort you've put into it, making the label can sometimes feel like a chore, but in many ways it is the icing on the cake, and it will allow your quilt to be identified in the future and become part of quilting history.

EIGHT

For the Novice

Success is not the key to happiness. Happiness is the key to success. If you love what you are doing, you will be successful.

—ALBERT SCHWEITZER

This chapter provides resources to help the novice quilter. We will discuss classes, books, magazines, websites, and kits. All of these resources can help you get started with quilting on your own, even if you don't know anyone else with whom to quilt or from whom to learn.

Classes

When I first started to quilt, I tried to learn from books and magazines. I didn't know anyone who quilted, and I didn't know that there were such things as quilt classes, bees, guilds, retreats, and university classes.

My first attempt at quilting was a large bed-sized quilt made from pieces of percale sheets, a dress I'd sewn for my then-husband's graduation, and leftover fabric from a shirt he had made. While I'm still quite proud of my color choices and the overall design of the quilt (I designed it myself based on a pattern I saw in a book), the execution left a lot to be desired! None of my points matched. My sashings were crooked. All in all, it was pretty sad.

The quilt top is still just a top because at the time I had no idea how to "quilt" a quilt. The piecing was easy (well, matching the blocks up was not, but assembling them was), but the whole concept of quilting the layers together was beyond me. I decided quilting was not for me. That was in 1995 or so.

> A sashing in a quilt is just like a window sashing. It is a piece that runs horizontally or vertically (or both) around the quilt blocks just like window sashings frame the panes of glass in a window.

In 1997 I moved to Grand Rapids, Michigan, from New Brunswick, Canada. Shortly after Christmas I went to the mall. I walked past a small shop with a sign outside that said Quilting Classes. I was thrilled. I walked in and was greeted by a friendly, bubbly woman named Pam. The shop was called Grand Quilt and it was like paradise for a "fabricoholic" like me. It was full of bright fun colors and lots of gorgeous quilts. I had never seen actual quilting fabric before—just boring calicos. I was completely enthralled by the batiks! I can't remember if I signed up immediately or on a later visit, but I do know that by my second or third visit the staff knew me by name and welcomed me, crooked sashings and all!

My first class was a Celtic appliqué class with Beth Ann Williams. I was shy and nervous and chose light blue and dark blue as my colors. Not very daring, but at least that sort of color combination has a name (analogous) and is a legitimate design choice. (Not that I knew that then. I was embarrassed that I couldn't find better colors . . . And I don't even like blue!)

Beth Ann was the soul of patience with me and the other newbie quilters. She told us more than we could ever possibly absorb about how to prepare our fabric, how to cut, how to appliqué by machine, what threads and needles to use, and a myriad other hints and tips that would only sink in much later. I finished my little wall hanging and actually quilted it (although only enough to hold the knotwork in place).

Thus began my love affair with quilting.

Over the next few years, as I moved to another part of the city and the shop moved to a new, self-contained storefront, I took many more classes from Beth Ann, and her contagious love of the craft not only wore off on me, but infected me totally. I learned about Celtic history, color theory, African, Asian, and Australian fabrics and some of the stories behind them. I learned to machine appliqué and machine quilt and how to make a wide assortment of different quilt patterns and styles, including tiny postcard "quilts." Sometimes Beth taught from existing books or patterns, and sometimes she just taught us techniques and let us play with the fabric. Eventually, she began publishing her own books and we learned from them. (I have listed some of Beth's books in the Resources section in case you want to learn more.)

I took a class in hand appliqué and one in "quilt-as-you-go" from other teachers, but always went back to Beth's classes because she is the best teacher in the world (in my humble opinion!). She makes you feel like you can do anything. Every design decision you make is right—because you are the artist, and it was your decision. Her support and encouragement really fed my love of the art, and I hope that every one of you might be lucky enough to find a teacher like her at least once in your life.

So seek out a class! Don't be shy; dive right in. If you happen to find a teacher who seems stuck in a rut or who tells you that you *must* do it exactly as the pattern says, find a new teacher. Quilting is not meant to be a chore or an exercise in frustration.

Like any other art, it should help you to relax and put you "in the zone." When I'm designing a new quilt, hours can slip past without my even noticing. I had to put a huge clock in my sewing room just so I'd remember to eat supper!

You can find classes at just about any quilt shop and many ordinary fabric shops. Many colleges and universities have adult education classes in quilting. Many quilt guilds offer classes, and, if all else fails, find a quilt bee full of kind people and ask for help. If there is one thing that quilters love to do, it is tell other people how to quilt. They share tips, tricks, patterns, and stories. Countless times, while quilting with a group, I have run into a snag in my project and thought all was lost, but showing it to my friends and getting their input almost always provided me with a new way to proceed, and a project I thought was lost suddenly took on new life.

Books

I have seventy-one books in my quilting studio. All of them tell me how to make quilts of various kinds. You can find quilting books almost anywhere—the library, the quilt shop, the fabric shop, and online at any bookseller or commercial quilt-related website.

In my opinion, the best books for beginners are those that give simple (yet thorough) instructions, and several inspiring (though easy) quilt patterns. Here are a few I like:

General Reference

- *The Quilter's Pocket Reference: An Easy Guide to Yardage and More* by Peggy Scholley. This tiny book has everything you need to know about tedious measurements and common tasks.

- *The Quilter's Quick Reference Guide* by Candace Eisner Strick. This is another small but helpful book. It covers everything from color theory to hand appliqué.

The following books from the Singer company are excellent reference books. They have inspiring pictures and very easy-to-follow instructions for machine quilting.

- Singer Quilting by Machine

- Singer Quilted Projects and Garments

- Singer Quilt Projects by Machine

Specific Tasks

Borders can be tricky, and sometimes you fall into a rut of making the same border over and over again. *The Border Workbook* by Janet Kime and *Happy Endings* by Mimi Dietrich will inspire you! If you want something more elaborate, try the ideas in *Interlacing Borders: More Than 100 Intricate Designs Made Easy* by Donna Hussain.

Dying your own quilting fabric is a great way to express yourself and make your quilts unique. *Hand-Dyed Fabric Made Easy* by Adriene Buffington and *Dying to Quilt: Quick Direct-Dye Methods for Quilt Makers* by Joyce Mori and Cynthia Myerberg are two of my favorite how-to books.

Related to dying, fabric painting is another fun option. *Color Moves: Transfer Paints on Fabric* by Linda Kemshall is another good book for the adventurous quilter.

Embellishing quilts is also a thrill for many quilters. *The Stori of Beaded Embellishment* by Mary Stori is a classic in that regard.

Machine appliqué is a passion of mine, and my very favorite series of appliqué patterns are by Nancy Halvorsen in her *Art to*

Heart series. Her patterns are easy, fun, and whimsical and she has something for every season and occasion. You can buy them at quilt shops or from her website: www.arttoheart.com/online/index.html.

As I mentioned, the first quilt I ever completed was a Celtic quilt and I learned from the best. Beth Ann Williams's *Celtic Quilts: A New Look for Ancient Designs* will tell you everything you need to know to make gorgeous Celtic interlace appliqué by machine. Another great Celtic-design book is *Celtic Spirals* by Philomena Durcan.

For the more artistic among you, here are a few books that are each in a category of their own:

- *Focus on Features* by Charlotte Warr Anderson teaches you how to make lifelike human and animal faces using elaborate appliqué.

- *Quilted Landscapes: Machine-Embellished Fabric Images* by Joan Blalock will bring out your inner landscape artist.

- *Personal Imagery in Art Quilts* by Erika Carter will show you how you can use simple quilting techniques to make a unique piece of art.

- *Post Cards: Make and Mail* by Cheryl Haynes, Barbara Cooley, and Beth Davis shows you how to make quick, fun postcard-sized quilts that can actually be sent through the mail.

- *Color for the Terrified Quilter: Plain Talk, Simple Lessons, 11 Projects* by Ionne McCauley and Sharon Pederson. This book will help you gain confidence in choosing color schemes for your quilts.

- Finally, *Hand Quilting with Alex Anderson: Six Projects for Hand Quilters* will let you give your machine a rest and help you perfect your hand stitch!

Magazines

There are dozens of great quilt-related magazines available. There are some with very basic, simple quilt patterns; many with intermediate patterns; and some that focus on different types of quilts, such as art quilts or appliqué. There is even a magazine for quilters that does not focus on quilt patterns and techniques, but on all the other things a quilter has going on in his or her life. Here is a list of my favorite quilt magazines. Most of these are available on the newsstand, but if you can't find them locally, check out an online bookstore.

- *McCall's Quilting*
- *Quilter's Newsletter*
- *American Quilter*
- *Quilter's Home*
- *American Patchwork and Quilting*

Websites

There are literally millions of quilt-related websites. I just did a Google search using the word "quilting" and got 2, 070,000 English-language pages. It would take years to even view them all, much less look at the content. How do you narrow it down? How can you find the ones that are right for you? The ones that tell you want you want to know?

First, decide what you hope to get out of it. This will help you narrow your search terms. The phrase "quilt pattern" returned hundreds of thousands of pages. (Too many for me!) The phrase "quilt block pattern" returned 16,300 pages. The phrase "appliqué quilt block pattern" returned just 16 pages. Now *that* is a manageable number to look through.

So if you are searching for websites, try to use the most narrow, targeted search terms you can. This will save you time and sanity.

Kits

Kit quilts were very popular in the early- to mid-1900s. Nowadays, many quilt shops design their own quilt kits, which normally include the pattern and precut fabrics to create the quilt blocks. Sometimes they also include sashings if the pattern calls for them, and backing fabric. If you are afraid that you can't choose good colors or won't be able to cut a straight line, a kit may be for you.

Another variation on kit quilts is the block-of-the-month quilt. Many shops and quilting websites feature a different block each month. Normally you pay a small fee the first month and receive the fabric and pattern for one block. One block per month is a manageable project, even for a novice quilter. If you run into problems, the shop will usually help you figure it out. When you bring the completed block back, you get the next month's kit, including a new pattern and fabrics.

I did the block-of-the-month at Grand Quilt the year they did blue and yellow quilts. I bought a new machine halfway through the year and did not think to check my quarter-inch seam allowances. So half my blocks were twelve inches . . . and half were somewhat smaller. When I tried to make my quilt at the end of the year, I ended up making two twin-size quilts instead of one large one. But since I completed my block every month I only had to pay $5 for the first pattern, and all the other patterns and fabrics were free. (I did have to buy sashings, but even that fabric was on sale so I got a great deal.) And no, before you ask, these quilts are not quilted either . . . Someday, though!

NINE

Keeping It Fun

A playful path is the shortest road to happiness.

—ANONYMOUS

So now that you are an experienced quilter (you did work your way through chapter seven, didn't you?), how can you keep it fun? How can you share your love of quilting with others? Where can you even find other quilters with whom you can share ideas? How can you stay mindful of the spiritual aspects of creating quilted art?

I hope this chapter will be a jumping-off point for new and experienced quilters alike. I want to encourage you to explore novel ways of creating quilts and inspire you to discover and develop your own unique creative voice while sharing this joy with others.

Most quilters enjoy the company of other quilters. Sometimes we just need to talk to someone who understands our obsession with fabric or thread or whatever it is that thrills us about quilting. Also, as a new quilter, you have thousands of questions, large and small, about how to do this or that. Where do you turn?

Many people are too hard on themselves when they start a creative endeavor like quilting. They think they are doing it "wrong," or that they will never get a perfect seam or a mitered border "just right." Relax: there are no Quilt Police, and unless you plan to enter shows and have to worry about judges, no one has to love your quilt but you. Sometimes you need supportive friends who have been there and done that to remind you of this fact.

I know we all want praise and adoration. We all want to think that someone else somewhere thinks our work is beautiful (or at least worth our time and effort). But, really—who cares what others think, as long as your quilts make you happy and bring you pleasure? Genius is never appreciated in its own time, as they say. So quilt the way you want, enjoy the process, and the outcome will be perfect in its own way.

So the first thing to do, if you want companionship with other quilters and a nonjudgmental atmosphere in which to work on your newfound (or longtime) creative passion, is to find a group of like-minded quilters and ask them very nicely if you may join their bee, sewing group, stitch-and-bitch, or whatever they call it. A good place to start is at the local quilt shop. Many of them have their own established bees and may be accepting new members. If they are not currently open to new members, then they can probably direct you to a bee that is open.

If this leads nowhere, find a local quilt guild. A quick search on the Internet can reveal a long list of guilds, and every one of them will have some kind of bee or other sewing group (or several). Find a local guild, call or e-mail them, and see if they know of any bees that are taking new members. If not, join the guild anyway.

Quilt guilds come in all types and sizes. Some are tiny and just starting out. Some have been around for decades. Some do char-

ity work exclusively, while others do some charity work and also other fun events. Some hold shows, have guest speakers, organize shop hops, host libraries of quilt-related books and videos, and host bees and other smaller quilting groups within them.

Like any organization, some are friendlier than others. Some have different points of view or opinions, but if you look around, chances are you can find one that's a good fit for you, or at least a group of people within the guild itself with whom you have something in common. Every guild I've been to has welcomed new members and been very appreciative of the interest shown in them.

To find a list of guilds, visit quiltguilds.com. This handy site lists guilds all around the world! It is where I found out about the Berrien Towne & Country Quilters' Guild, which I joined in early 2007. This group of about 170 women in southwestern Michigan meets ten times a year and sponsors many small quilting groups within its membership, as well as a biannual show on even-numbered years. This site also lists my former guild, West Michigan Quilters' Guild. This group has over 400 members, is very active in the community, and donates all profits (and hundreds of quilts) to charity each year. It also hosts a show every even-numbered year.

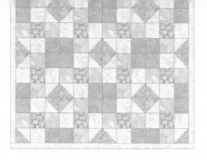

Glossary

Quilting, like any other craft or art form, has many terms that are unique to it. Some of these are defined here. If you cannot locate the definition of a word you do not understand, an online glossary of quilting terms can be found at quilting.about.com.

$1/4$-inch Foot: A special attachment for your sewing machine. It features a guide that assists in maintaining a consistent seam. A consistent seam allowance is vital if your blocks are to piece together correctly.

Analogous: Any group of colors that lie together on a color wheel are said to be analogous, such as blue-green, green, and yellow-green.

Appliqué: Involves cutting out shapes and sewing them down on top of a background fabric. This can be done by hand or machine, and often involves the use of a stabilizer to give the background more body. Appliqué is often used alone, but may be combined with piecework.

Backing: This is the back of the quilt and is normally made of the same weight and grade of cotton as the front. It may be plain, or patterned fabric. Small quilts can be backed with one piece of material, while larger quilts require pieced backs. Some quilts are reversible, with the backing being as intricate as the top.

Basting: Describes the steps taken to hold the three layers of the quilt sandwich together. It can be done with thread, safety pins, or basting spray. It is necessary to prevent the top and back from shifting or bunching during quilting.

Batting: The middle layer of a quilt that provides warmth and thickness. It can be made of cotton, cotton/polyester blend, wool, or silk.

Bearding: The gradual process of batting fibers poking through the fabric. Using bonded or needlepunched battings will lessen this problem.

Bias: A forty-five-degree line across the grain of the fabric. Fabric that is cut on the bias is prone to stretching, so care must be taken when sewing bias edges.

Bias Binding: This is a type of binding which is cut on the bias of the fabric. It has some stretch and give to it and so is useful on quilts that have curved edges.

Binding: The edge treatment that surrounds the quilt. It encloses the raw edges of the backing, batting and top. It is usually at least two layers thick. This provides protection from wear and tear along the edges of the quilt.

Butted Seams: Seams that meet and must be pressed close together —so that the seams line up properly on top. This is necessary in most types of pieced blocks where shapes come together.

Chain Piecing: In this method of piecing, you feed pairs of shapes into the sewing machine one after another, leaving a short "chain" of thread between them. When you are done with those shapes, you clip them apart at the chains, press them, align them with the next piece they have to match and repeat the process. This is much faster, and uses less thread than piecing one entire block at a time.

Channel Quilting: Involves sewing a series of straight lines side by side across the quilt, either horizontally or vertically. You may use the guide on your walking foot to space your stitching lines, or you can use lengths of masking tape to guide you.

Complementary Color: Colors that appear opposite each other on the color wheel, such as red and green.

Cool Color: Any color with a short wavelength. Cool colors always contain blue.

Couched down: Couching refers to creating a design on the surface of fabric by laying down a thread and fastening it with small, evenly spaced stitches. This is a form of embellishment that is often used on quilted garments.

Dual Needle: Some sewing machines come equipped with a dual needle, which is an attachment with two needles side-by-side. This can be used for special effects, such as sewing parallel rows with two different colored threads.

Echo Quilting: Similar to channel quilting, echo quilting involves quilting concentric lines around a shape so that the quilting echoes the shape. Echo quilting is normally done in lines that are $\frac{1}{4}$ inch to $\frac{1}{2}$ inch apart.

Electric Quilt: A computer program distributed by the Electric Quilting Company. It allows you to design quilts and quilt blocks on the screen and see how they will look with specific fabrics before buying or cutting the material. For more information, go to electricquilt.com.

Fat Quarter: This is a quarter yard of fabric that is created by cutting a half yard of fabric in half horizontally. This yields a wider piece of fabric (18 inches by 22 inches) from which to cut strips or appliqué shapes.

Finished: In quilting, "finished size" is the size of a quilt block after it has been pieced into a quilt. It does not take the seam allowances into account.

Free-Motion Foot (Darning Foot, Embroidery Foot): A special attachment for your sewing machine that allows you to create intricate quilting designs. The feed dogs of the machine are either lowered or covered up, and you move the fabric freely with your hands rather than relying on the feed dogs to move it.

Free-Motion Quilting: This kind of quilting is created using a free-motion or darning foot. Using this method, you can create stippling, or meandering patterns, or draw on the fabric with the thread creating words or shapes. It is an excellent way to fill in large open areas. Because the stitching is normally close together, this technique uses a lot of thread and can cause the quilt to shrink in size.

Freezer Paper: Paper, waxed on one side and usually sold in grocery stores. Intended for wrapping meat for the freezer, this paper is used by quilters for making templates and appliqué patterns.

Half-Square Triangles: These are composed of two right triangles. They can be made by cutting and piecing the triangles together (which increases the difficulty), or by using the grid method, as described in the text.

Hand: Describes the feel of a fabric and the way it drapes.

In the Ditch: Quilting in the ditch means quilting in the grooves where two pieces of fabric are pieced together. This is one of the simplest ways to quilt straight lines and allows the quilting to disappear so that the fabrics and shapes become the focus of the piece.

Lapped Borders: Also called butted or squared borders. One part of the border is lapped over the other.

Mitered Borders: A miter is the edge of a piece where a joint is made by cutting two pieces at an angle and fitting them together. These borders are more difficult to master than lapped borders, but are well worth the effort.

Monochromatic: A color scheme in which many shades of the same color are used.

Monofilament Thread: This type of thread is made from a single strand of nylon. It is frequently used for machine appliqué. It is not as chemical and UV resistant as other types of thread, but has the advantage of disappearing into the quilt top, making your appliqué appear to float on the surface of the quilt.

Muslin: A plain, usually undyed cotton fabric, available bleached or unbleached. It is available in a wide range of qualities and is the foundation for all patterned cotton fabrics. Fine quality bleached muslin is often used in quilting as a neutral background for appliqué or as a foundation under thinner fabric.

Nine-Patch: A block made up of nine smaller blocks. It is a simple and standard block used in quilting.

Piecing: The technique of sewing together different shapes to create a quilt block, and eventually, a quilt top.

Presser Foot: The attachment on a sewing machine that presses down on the fabric as it moves under the needle. Necessary for maintaining proper tension on the fabric so that the stitches don't pucker.

Quilt Clips: Metal clips that hold a quilt in a rolled-up fashion during machine quilting—helps you to control larger quilts.

Quilt Frame: Any device that holds the quilt layers taut so that they may be easily quilted. Quilt frames can be made of many materials, including wood and plastic. John Flynn has designed a special quilt frame that may be used with an ordinary home sewing machine. You can get more information at flynnquilt.com.

Quilt Sandwich: The three layers of a quilt: the top, the batting, and the backing.

Quilt-As-You-Go (Block by Block, Lap Quilting): In this technique, you piece each block directly onto the batting and backing. This allows you to quilt it as you go because each piecing seam becomes a quilting seam. It is especially suited to patterns such as Log Cabin, with lots of long, straight seams, but can be adapted to a variety of blocks.

Retayne: A commercially available detergent. It is used to set or fix the color in commercially dyed cotton fabrics.

Rotary Cutter: A very sharp circular cutter, resembling a pizza cutter.

It is used for cutting through layers of quilt fabric. It is normally used with a special mat to protect the surface under the blade.

Rotary Cutting: Performed with a rotary cutter and mat, this technique makes cutting a large number of strips or blocks very easy.

Rotary Cutting Mat: A special mat, (usually made of self-healing material) used for rotary cutting.

Rotary Ruler: A special ruler—normally transparent—used for rotary cutting. Most have 45- and 60-degree angles on them, in addition to the standard $\frac{1}{8}$-inch, $\frac{1}{4}$-inch, and $\frac{1}{2}$-inch markings.

Scant $\frac{1}{4}$-inch Seam: The most common seam allowance in quilting is the scant $\frac{1}{4}$-inch seam. Scant means that the seam is just barely less than $\frac{1}{4}$ inch; about a thread narrower than a full $\frac{1}{4}$ inch.

Selvage: The finished edge of the fabric. It sometimes contains information about the fabric such as manufacturer, designer name, etc. It is cut off before piecing.

Seminole Piecing: A machine-piecing technique developed by the Seminole and Miccosukee Indians of Florida in the 1800s. It features strips of fabric pieced together, cut on an angle, and then pieced again to form intricate patterns. It is often used to adorn clothing, but also makes wonderful quilt borders.

Serger: A type of sewing machine that creates a finished edge along the fabric. In quilting, it is sometimes used to bind the edges of the fabric before it is washed, in order to prevent unraveling.

Shade: A hue produced by adding black to a pure color.

Sliver Trim: A method of trimming fabric, quilt blocks, or quilt tops by taking a very narrow sliver of fabric off one or more edges. Normally done to square up a piece that has stretched or become distorted during piecing or quilting.

Square Ruler: Used for squaring up quilts and quilt blocks, square rulers come in a variety of sizes. The best ones have a diagonal line running from one corner to the other to assist in the squaring process.

Square Up: Each block must be perfectly squared in order for them to fit consistently together.

Stash: A stash is a quilter's collection of fabric. It may also include thread, batting, and notions.

Straight of Grain: The straight of grain runs parallel to the selvage of a piece of fabric.

Synthrapol: A commercially available detergent that removes excess dye from hand-dyed fabrics, including commercially available batiks and hand dyes. It also keeps this dye from redepositing on the fabric or on other materials washed along with it.

Take Up: This phrase refers to the phenomena of a quilt shrinking as it is quilted. This happens most frequently on heavily quilted pieces. Basically, the tight quilting causes the entire quilt sandwich to grow smaller than it originally was. This is something to consider when you plan your quilting design.

Tint: A hue produced by adding white to a pure color.

Tone: A hue produced by adding gray to a pure color.

Tone-On-Tone: Tone-on-tone describes a type of fabric where the same color is used more than once, in several different shades, or tones. These fabrics are useful for helping blend disparate colors and also for the plainer background areas of a design.

Triad: A triad is any three hues that are equally positioned on a color wheel, such as green, orange, and purple.

Usable Fabric Width: Because fabric has two selvage edges, the actual width of fabric that you can use is less than that advertised. For example, 45-inch-wide fabric normally yields only about 42 or 43 inches of usable fabric width after it has been washed. The rest is selvage and must be discarded.

Walking Foot (Even feed foot): A special attachment for a sewing machine that helps feed the quilt layers through more evenly. The underside of the walking foot has feed dogs that pull the top of the quilt along at the same rate that the feed dogs on the machine pull the bottom. It is very useful for quilting in the ditch or for quilting straight or gently curved patterns. It can also be used when piecing for extra accuracy.

Warm Color: Colors with long wavelengths, like red.

APPENDIX A

Resources

Books

Arnett, William, Alvia Wardlaw, Jane Livingston, John Beardsley. *The Quilts of Gee's Bend*. Tinwood Books, 2002.

Singer Sewing Reference Library. *Quilting by Machine*. Creative Publishing International, Inc., 1990.

Baatz, Barbara. *Iron-On Transfers for Quilt Labels*. American School of Needlework, 1999.

Ban Breathnach, Sarah. *Simple Abundance Journal of Gratitude*. New York: Warner Books Inc., 1996. Sarah's books, including *A Daybook of Comfort and Joy* and *Something More* are well-loved and much-read companions in my house. Sarah's outlook on life is the antidote I needed to my too-hectic and stressed-out lifestyle.

Beardsley, John, William Arnett, Paul Arnett, Jane Livingston. *Gee's Bend: The Women and Their Quilts*. Atlanta, GA. Tinwood Books, 2002.

Colby, Averil. *Quilting*. New York: Charles Scribner's Sons, 1971.

McCauley, Daniel, and Kathryn McCauley. *Decorative Arts of the Amish of Lancaster County*. Intercourse, PA: Good Books, 1988.

McHaney Danner, Ruth, and Cristine Bolley. *What I Learned from God While Quilting*. Barbour Publishing, Inc., 2003. Each chapter includes a true story on a quilt-related theme, followed by "The Quilting Frame" (a spiritual application), "God's Template" (a relevant Scripture), "The

Binding Stitch" (a brief prayer), and the "Scrap Bag" (a practical quilting tip).

Nerud, Thea. *One-of-a-Kind Quilt Labels: Unique Ideas for a Special Finishing Touch.* Martingale & Company, 2004.

Pritchard, Gayle A. *Uncommon Threads.* Ohio: Ohio University Press. This book reveals the story of the roots of art quilting in the United States. See ohioswallow.com/book/Uncommon+Threads to read reviews on this book and to order it. Be sure to check out the "Image Gallery" to view some fantastic art quilts; they're a sampling of the fascinating quilts you will see in the book.

Rogers, Penelope Walton. "Cotton in a Merovingian Burial in Germany." *Archaeological Textiles Newsletter* #27 (Autumn 1998).

Staniland, Kay. *Medieval Craftsmen Embroiderers.* Toronto: University of Toronto Press, 1991.

Tatem, Mary. *The Quilt of Life: A Patchwork of Devotional Thoughts.* Barbour Publishing, Inc., 2000. This book contains ninety "devotional vignettes— all centered on a quilting theme—that follow the process of God's work in our lives."

Tobin, Jacqueline L., and Raymond G. Dobard. *Hidden in Plain View: A Secret Story of Quilts and the Underground Railroad.* Anchor, 2000. At one time it was believed that former slaves and others in the United States used quilt blocks as codes to reveal safe houses and paths along the Underground Railroad. This book is one of the best-known books on the subject, though the story was later debunked. See ugrrquilt.hartcottage-quilts.com by Leigh Fellner for detailed information on more recent research into this story.

Towner-Larsen, Susan. *Within Sacred Circles.* Pilgrim Press, The United Church Press, 2004.

Williams, Beth Ann. *Celtic Quilts: A New Look for Ancient Designs.* Martingale & Company, 2000.

Williams, Beth Ann. *A World of Quilts: 10 Projects Using Ethnic Fabrics.* Martingale & Company, 2003.

Winston, Kimberly. *Fabric of Faith: A Guide to the Prayer Quilt Ministry.* Morehouse Publishing, 2006. This book describes step by step how to make a prayer quilt.

Websites

For information about threads, visit amefird.com. This company makes many popular quilting threads.

The Michigan State University Museum Quilt Center is one of many institutions that works to collect and preserve quilt history: museum.msu.edu/glqc/.

For information on color theory, see worqx.com/color/index.htm.

You can see some beautiful examples of molas at galenfrysinger.com/mola_panama.htm.

Calvin Coolidge's quilt: historicvermont.org/coolidge/CoolidgeBrigadoon.html.

For information on quilting in Hawaii, visit quiltshawaii.com.

Nice-To-Know Info

Batting, threads, and needles are necessary for quilting, but how can new quilters know what kind they need? This appendix will give you a lot of great information on what kind of batting to use, what size needles and threads go together, and provide you with a quick reference.

Batting

Battings (the filling of the quilt) can be bonded or needle-punched. Both of these processes are intended to prevent bunching or bearding of the fibers in the batting. According to *Quilting by Machine,* different battings have the following characteristics.

Fiber Content	Appearance of Finished Quilt	Characteristics	Spacing of Quilting Stitches
Cotton	Flat	Absorbs moisture, cool in summer, warm in winter	½" to 1" (1.3–2.5 cm)
Polyester	Puffy	Warmth and loft without weight, nonallergenic, moth & mildew-resistant	3" to 5" (7.5–12.5 cm)
Cotton/ Poly Blend	Moderately flat	Combines characteristics of cotton and polyester	2" to 4" (5–10 cm)

Batting Lofts

Loft refers to the thickness of the batting. If you want an antique appearance to your quilt, you would use a batting with less loft. If you want your quilting to be emphasized, you would choose a high-loft batting. Thicker loft battings are usually warmer than thin loft battings. According to *Quilting by Machine*, the following are the standard thicknesses, or lofts, of common battings.

Low-loft	$\frac{1}{8}$" to $\frac{3}{8}$"	(3 mm to 1 cm)
Medium-loft	$\frac{1}{2}$" to $\frac{3}{4}$"	(1.3 to 2 cm)
High-loft	1" to 2"	(2.5 to 5 cm)
Extra-high-loft	2" to 3"	(5 to 7.5 cm)

Packaged Batting Sizes

The table below shows the standard sizes of packaged battings.

Crib	45" x 60"	(115 x 152.5 cm)
Twin	72" x 90"	(183 x 229 cm)
Full (Double)	81" x 96"	(206 x 244 cm)
Queen	90" x 108"	(229 x 274.5 cm)
King	120" x 120"	(305 x 305 cm)

Thread Size

According to the American and Efird website (amefird.com), "Many different thread size systems are used in the world for sewing threads. Generally, the thread size refers to the diameter or thickness of the thread. American and Efird, Inc., uses the Tex Size universally for all of its thread products. Other thread ticket size systems used include the Cotton Count System (60/3), the Metric System (120's), the Denier System (100d X 3) and the Silk System used for both Silk and Mercerized Cotton threads (000/3). Larger thread sizes are generally used on heavier fabrics. They are usually stronger and provide greater seam strength. Heavier sizes are more expensive and will cause more bobbin changes on lockstitch machines." American and Efird produce a number of well-known quilting threads including Mettler, Robison-Anton, and YKK.

Thread holds your piecing together, quilts your top to your batting and backing, and is also used for embellishing the quilt top. Below, you will find common machine-quilting threads, and their characteristics and uses.

Types and Uses of Threads

Material	Use
Cotton	A good all-purpose thread that can be used for piecing or quilting. Not as strong as mercerized cotton.
Mercerized Cotton	Mercerizing is a process that strengthens the thread and increases the luster and depth of the dye color. Mercerized cotton has a slight sheen to it and is very strong. This is my preferred thread for piecing.
Polyester & Cotton/Poly blends	These threads are strong, but some quilters assert that the polyester will, over time, cut through the delicate cotton fibers of the quilt and destroy it.
Rayon	Rayon threads are very shiny and beautiful, but not as strong as the cotton threads. They are often used on wall hangings and other decorative objects, which will not be frequently washed, or subject to wear.
Nylon Monofilament	Used for machine appliqué and for quilting that you want to make "disappear" into the top. Monofilament thread is very thin. It is used only on the top, *never* in the bobbin, as the winding of the bobbin will take away its stretch and flexibility, making it brittle and prone to breakage.

Silk	Very rarely used for machine quilting due to its delicate nature, silk thread is a natural fiber with a high sheen. It is quite beautiful when used for hand appliqué.
Metallic	Metallic threads can add sparkle to holiday quilts and quilted clothing. They must be used with special sewing machine needles designed for metallic thread, as regular needles will cause the thread to shred and break.
Specialty	Specialty threads can include chenille, silk ribbon, lamé, cords, beaded cords and many other types of commercially available or handmade yarns and threads. These are used for embellishing and may be couched down by machine, but are not fed through the machine itself.

APPENDIX C

Online Quilt Shops

I do most of my fabric shopping at my local quilt shops, where I can see the true colors and actually touch the fabrics (because, let's face it, fondling the fabric is 90 percent of the fun). But if you don't have a local quilt shop, or if you get a hankering for a fat quarter late at night, here are a few shops that sell high-quality fabrics via the Internet. I'm sure there are plenty more, but these are the ones I personally know about.

- keepsakequilting.com—The online shop of a beautiful brick-and-mortar quilt shop in New Hampshire. Keepsake Quilting also has a beautiful mail-order catalog.

- equilter.com—One of my favorite online shops, eQuilter is run by Luana and Paul Rubin. Their weekly newsletter is always full of gorgeous new fabrics and an update on their latest travels. eQuilter is an online-only shop.

- bighornquilts.com—This is another favorite online shop. They have a good selection and their "real life" shop is located in Greybull, Wyoming.

- hancocks-paducah.com—Hancock's of Paducah is known to any quilter who has ever been to the American Quilter's Society show in Paducah, Kentucky. Their shop is huge with good prices and an incredible selection.

- yoderdepartmentstore.com—Yoder Department Store in Shipshewana, Indiana, is a treasure trove of unique items. Their fabric department has a wide assortment of fabrics, and they are now selling them online, too.

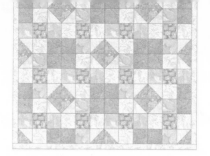

Index

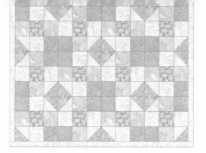

About the Author

Kelly Smith is a writer and IT consultant who has been quilting for more than ten years. She has taught friends and their children how to machine appliqué and make small quilting projects like tote bags and pillows. Twice a year she attends a four-day quilt retreat with more than thirty other women, where they share ideas and inspiration. She regularly attends classes to learn new techniques and to network, and she enjoys designing quilts from scratch, or using a published pattern as a jumping off point to create her own masterpieces.

You can visit Kelly's website at www.redheadedquilter.com.